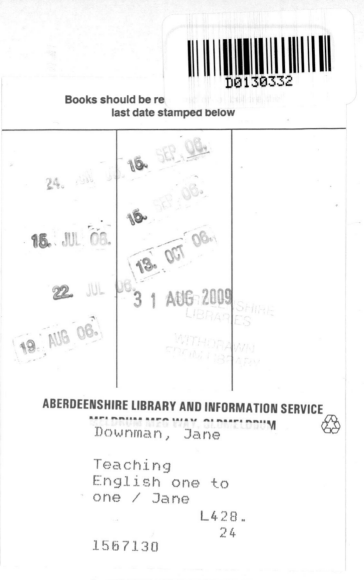

teach® yourself

teaching english
one to one

jane downman and
john shepheard

The **teach yourself** series does
exactly what it says, and it works.
For over 60 years, more than
40 million people have learnt over
750 subjects the **teach yourself**
way, with impressive results.

be where you want to be
with **teach yourself**

For UK orders: please contact Bookpoint Ltd, 130 Milton Park, Abingdon, Oxon OX14 4SB. Telephone: +44 (0) 1235 827720. Fax: +44 (0) 1235 400454. Lines are open from 09.00–18.00, Monday to Saturday, with a 24-hour message answering service. You can also order through our website www.madaboutbooks.co.uk

For USA order enquiries: please contact McGraw-Hill Customer Services, PO Box 545, Blacklick, OH 43004-0545, USA. Telephone: 1-800-722-4726. Fax: 1-614-755-5645.

For Canada order enquiries: please contact McGraw-Hill Ryerson Ltd., 300 Water St, Whitby, Ontario L1N 9B6, Canada. Telephone: 905 430 5000. Fax: 905 430 5020.

Long renowned as the authoritative source for self-guided learning – wit' the *Teach You* Downman, Jane of languages, cr on.

British Librar Teaching English ue record for this one to one /

Library of Con Jane Downman and

First publishe L428. 38 Euston Road,

24

First published on of the McGra 1567130 ist Randolph Stre

This edition published 2003.

The 'Teach Yourself' name and logo are registered trade marks of Hodder & Stoughton Ltd.

Typeset by Transet Limited, Coventry
Printed in Great Britain for Hodder & Stoughton Educational, a division of Hodder Headline Ltd, 338 Euston Road, London NW1 3BH by Cox & Wyman Ltd, Reading, Berkshire.

Impression number   10 9 8 7 6 5 4 3 2
Year   2007 2006 2005 2004 2003

contents

information transfer, summaries,
transformations and visual input

- making use of these techniques
without a computer

acknowledgements

For my mother and father, with love and gratitude

JD

For mum

JS

The authors would like to thank the following for their assistance in the preparation of this book:

Catherine Downman; Haiyin Mai; Kazuya Matsumoto; Thomas Meili; Heather Roberts; Shiori Sakashita; Robert Taylor; Max Thompson; André Verazzo.

Thanks to Robin Summers and David Anthonisz of Global Village, London/Bromley School of English, where a good deal of one-to-one teaching experience was gained.

Thanks to Nick Wright for his thinking.

Thanks, too, go to Peter Wilberg for original inspiration.

preface

Why and who for?

This book has been written in response to a growing need for one-to-one teachers. It is not only aimed at experienced and qualified teachers, however; we hope that there is sufficient guidance for those who have not taught English before, but who find themselves in a situation where their knowledge of the language means that they can help others to learn it.

Included in the book is a variety of ideas and techniques, from which teachers can pick and choose those which most appeal. We hope that teachers will be inspired by these ideas and build on them.

Other ELT books

We have generally avoided covering aspects of teaching which are discussed in other books, of which there are very many – both for use in the classroom and as resources for teachers. However, where relevant, we have included suggestions for ways of approaching reading and listening, for example, which are explored in more detail in other books. Useful books and other materials referred to in the text are listed on page 186.

Class books

There is no reason why books written for classes should not be used in a one-to-one teaching situation. Group or pair work would be carried out by the teacher and student

working together. At the same time we feel that many of the ideas in this book for teaching one student can be incorporated into class teaching.

His and hers

For convenience we have referred to the teacher as 'she' and the student 'he' throughout the book. The book, however, has not been written solely with this combination in mind.

introduction

Think about

What are:

a two advantages of teaching one student?
b two disadvantages?

Growth area

Teaching one to one is a growth area in language learning. There is an increasing number of students who have little time at their disposal and very specific language needs. Commonly these needs may be: an interest in English as a hobby, frequently for the purposes of travel, to meet job or study requirements, and for extra help with passing examinations. It seems to be more frequent for schools to offer one-to-one courses as a specific option or as a complement to class teaching. There is also a trend towards companies providing tuition for their employees on their own premises. Many teachers, of course, are in the business of offering private lessons outside a school or institutional context as a means of supplementing their income. Increasingly common are 'homestay' courses, where the teacher provides board and accommodation as well as a social programme and language lessons.

Employer restrictions

Some schools build into their teacher contracts a provision which disallows their staff from giving private lessons to students who are enrolled with them. Sometimes this 'ban' extends beyond the student's period of enrolment such that teachers are cautioned against giving private tuition to students for up to six months after they have completed studies at a school. The thinking behind this is that the school has invested time and money in attracting students only for them then to be poached by teachers. Teachers concerned about this issue may wish to consult their contracts.

Money

Teachers are not always confident when handling the business side of giving private lessons outside a school context. However, it is worth approaching this area as professionally and as systematically as possible. It is worth arranging an initial lesson with a student as an assessment. This is to see whether the teacher and student feel happy working together and to assess student needs. Thereafter, a series of lessons over a period of time can be agreed.

Clearly the teacher and student need to agree on a fee for a lesson or series of lessons. It is probably a good idea not to significantly undercut the 'going rate' for lessons in your area but to charge something around the local rate. Lessons are normally for a 60-minute period and the student will expect not a minute less than this, so avoid finishing early. It is also worth thinking about travel costs and including these in the fee where relevant.

There needs to be clarity over a 'no-show' policy so that if the student is unable to attend then he still has to pay for the lesson. An alternative system could be that a cancellation with less than 24 hours' notice requires full payment for the lesson. There also needs to be clear agreement on when and how to pay: the student could pay in advance for a series of lessons, as would normally happen in a school setting; or payment could be made at the end of each lesson.

Rewards

In whatever context, teaching one student has its rewards and its challenges. Rewards are:

• meeting the needs of a student in terms of his language requirements

- meeting the needs of a student in terms of the way in which he prefers to learn language and to approach tasks
- gaining insight into the way a language can be learned
- understanding how differently or similarly a language is learned by different students.

Challenges

- **Intensity**   This refers to the sheer intensity of working closely with one student where potentially both teacher and student are in the spotlight. There is no recourse to pair or group work to allow for variety of interaction and a breathing space. Strategies for coping in this area are looked at in Unit 10, Peopling and Placing the Room, where techniques for introducing virtual third parties and places are used to break intensity; Unit 7, Cuisenaire Rods, shows how the use of coloured rods takes the focus away from the student and teacher; Unit 2, The Work Space, looks at options for easing the intensity through seating and related issues.

- **Gobbling the material**   There may be a need to prepare more tasks and materials for teaching one student than for working with a whole class. Some teachers find that they need twice as much material when working one to one. We will be looking at ways of slowing down the consumption of activities and materials and reworking language from different angles in Unit 5, Reformulation, including task repetition and rephrasing student-initiated language. These techniques provide ways of improving accuracy and sophistication of language use through reworking of material.

- **What exactly are the student's needs?**   When students request private lessons, they are sometimes vague about their objectives. They will often say they simply want to improve their English or they will ask for conversation lessons without any clear idea of what that might entail. Even if they have a general idea that they need English for their job, they may not be aware of specifics. Unit 1, The First Lesson, looks at procedures for assessing a student's level, identifying specific language and skills needs, and how he prefers to learn.

- **High expectations**   Students sometimes have the idea that if they sign up for one-to-one lessons eight hours a day for three weeks, they will learn an enormous amount of English. Even with a few hours a week they might have unrealistically high expectations. Again, needs analysis is a way of looking specifically at what students are aiming for and at what can be achieved. They may need to be advised that an hour regularly can be more effective than several hours *en bloc*.

- **What if I don't get on with the student?** There will often be some aspect of the student's personality or behaviour that causes difficulty in getting along well. One way of coping is to consider that aspects which we dislike in others are often aspects of ourselves which we would rather ignore. A student's impatience with himself, which we find exasperating, could indicate that on some level we are similarly impatient with ourselves. This may help to engender empathy with the student.

01

the first lesson

In this unit you will learn
- how to identify your student's needs
- how to prepare a syllabus for your student

Think about

Which of the following would you consider the most useful in one-to-one teaching?

computer	radio	blank tapes
family photographs	dictionary	menu
black or white board	magazines	

The teacher provides:

- **paper** The student will probably bring stationery with him, but the teacher should be prepared to provide it if necessary.
- **pens and pencils (and sharpener and eraser)** Some students feel happier using a pencil, so that errors can be erased, rather than crossed out.
- **highlighter pen** for highlighting structures/lexis in texts etc.
- **water-based pens** for the **white board** or for writing on **reusable laminated strips** (see Unit 8). There is no reason why a board should not be used in one-to-one teaching: it provides variety, is reusable and some students may benefit psychologically from the knowledge that whatever is written on it is not permanent.
- **glue, Blu Tack, dry adhesive** for displaying materials.
- **dictionary** for the teacher and the student (e.g. *Collins Cobuild Learner's Dictionary, Oxford Advanced Learner's Dictionary, Oxford Wordpower Dictionary for Learners of English*).
- **newspapers and magazines** as sources of pictures for presenting lexis, for stimulating discussions; authentic texts to practise reading skills (see Unit 11, Reading and Listening).
- **leaflets, timetables, menus**, etc. as sources for reading tasks.
- **radio, television, video** as sources of authentic texts to practise listening skills (see Unit 11, Reading and Listening).
- **tape recorder/dictaphone, blank tapes** for recording the student and the teacher (see Unit 6, Coursebooks, Retrospective Coursebooks and Blank Tapes).
- **postcards, family and other photographs** for stimulating discussion (see Unit 10, Peopling and Placing the Room).
- **computer** for access to websites to find authentic texts and for printing out the student's work.
- **Cuisenaire rods** (see Unit 7, Cuisenaire Rods).

The student brings:

- **file** which can be divided into sections (skills, grammar, etc.).

- separate **vocabulary book** which could also be divided into sections (alphabetically, according to subject and so on).

- **company profile, brochures, reports**, etc. if the student is studying business English.

- **photographs of family, home**, etc. to help with vocabulary and stimulate speaking and writing skills.

> ## Think about
>
> What four pieces of information would help most in designing a scheme of work for a student?

Needs analysis

Needs analysis allows the teacher to find out *what* the student needs from the course in terms of topic areas for vocabulary, language, skills and functions. It also means that the teacher can discover *how* the student likes to learn.

The form that the needs analysis will take depends on how it is to be carried out. The teacher may want to ask the student questions and make her own notes or ask him to fill in a questionnaire. If he is to do this alone, the language used in the questionnaire will need to be kept simple. Rather than questions, there could be a series of statements with which the student is asked to agree or disagree.

There follow two versions of a needs analysis questionnaire on the next page.

Language diagnosis

As well as finding out what the student needs and wants from the course, the teacher also needs to know what level he is at, which are his strong and which his weak areas, so that a syllabus can be devised. There are several ways to do this.

The teacher can set a diagnostic test. This could take the form of questions of increasing difficulty. Such a test can be found in

NEEDS ANALYSIS

My name ....

My job ....

I am learning English because:

I like it...☐

I need to use English at work ....☐

I want to travel ....☐

I need it in order to study ....☐

I need to pass an English exam ....☐

I need to improve at school/university ....☐

other ....

When did you start studying English?

....

Who do you need to write to in English?

....

What do you need to write about?

....

Who do you need to talk to in English?

....

Do you need to talk on the telephone?

....

What do you need to talk about?

....

What do you need to read in English?

....

What situations do you need English in?

....

I want to practise:	✓✓✓	✓✓	✓	✗
speaking	☐	☐	☐	☐
listening	☐	☐	☐	☐
reading	☐	☐	☐	☐
writing	☐	☐	☐	☐
vocabulary	☐	☐	☐	☐
pronunciation	☐	☐	☐	☐
grammar	☐	☐	☐	☐

I like:

	✓✓✓	✓✓	✓	✗
language games	☐	☐	☐	☐
lessons outside the classroom	☐	☐	☐	☐
tests	☐	☐	☐	☐
reading English books	☐	☐	☐	☐
grammar exercises	☐	☐	☐	☐
speaking	☐	☐	☐	☐

My hobbies/interests are: ....

NEEDS ANALYSIS

Name: _____

Occupation: _____

How long have you been studying English? _____

What are your reasons for learning English? _____

_____

_____

What sort of situations do you need English for? _____

_____

_____

What do you think you most need to practise? (1 = a little, 5 = a lot)
- speaking   1 2 3 4 5
- listening   1 2 3 4 5
- reading   1 2 3 4 5
- writing   1 2 3 4 5
- pronunciation   1 2 3 4 5
- vocabulary   1 2 3 4 5
- grammar   1 2 3 4 5

What are your hobbies/interests? _____

_____

How far do you agree with the following statements?

I think language games can be a good way to learn a language.	1 2 3 4 5
I would like to do a test from time to time.	1 2 3 4 5
I like the teacher to correct all my mistakes.	1 2 3 4 5
I enjoy doing grammar exercises.	1 2 3 4 5
I enjoy reading English books and magazines.	1 2 3 4 5
I think lessons should always be in the classroom.	1 2 3 4 5

the Study Guide from *English Grammar in Use* by Raymond Murphy. Each question in the Study Guide is cross-referenced with a particular grammar unit. The book also provides examples of the form and function of structures and exercises in which to practise these.

First language interference

Even before meeting the student, the teacher can learn about the kinds of problems he might have with studying English. *Learner English* is an invaluable book, which gives information about the phonological and grammatical differences between the student's native language and English. More than 20 languages are dealt with. The book also provides a list of 'false friends' for each language and has information on how attitudes to language and learning vary from culture to culture.

One way of using the background information on the language is to prepare a worksheet which contains typical errors made by speakers of that language. The task for the learner is to try to correct the errors. The sentences can include errors of grammar, spelling, punctuation, and vocabulary. For example, here are some sentences which could be offered to a Turkish student:

1 *My father teacher.* (There is no independent verb *be* in Turkish.)
2 *Careful with that glass, it breaks.* (Different coverage of tenses and verb forms may result in the present simple being used for the *will* future.)
3 *I had written to Kemal last month but he hasn't replied.* (There may be a tendency to use the past perfect for what is perceived as distant past.)

An alternative is to offer both the correct and incorrect sentences. For example:

1 *My father teacher/is a teacher.*
2 *Careful with that glass, it'll break/it breaks.*
3 *I had written/I wrote to Kemal last month but he hasn't replied.*

Another option is to include a list of words which contain typical problem sounds. The teacher can get the student to read them aloud or, where possible, draw pictures for students to identify. For example, Portuguese learners confuse the vowel sounds in *rich* and *reach* because the closest equivalent in

Portuguese is somewhere between the two. Portuguese speakers could be given the following list of words to pronounce:

rich   *reach*
hit   *heat*
pill   *peel*

Starting from speaking

Cuisenaire rods (see Unit 7) or the 'something to talk about' cards (see Resources and Ideas Bank) are a useful prompt to encourage the student to speak. The teacher could make notes about the student's speaking skills while listening and/or recording him to do so later. She could make notes under the following headings: **accuracy, fluency, phonology, vocabulary range**.

A student who speaks very hesitantly but with great accuracy might benefit from working on fluency, without worrying so much about making mistakes. The syllabus will need to include plenty of speaking tasks. Conversely, the student who speaks fluently, but whose pronunciation makes understanding him difficult needs to concentrate on areas of phonology. Another student might have a vocabulary range which is restricted to his area of work, so he needs help increasing his social vocabulary.

Starting from writing

The teacher might also want the student to do a piece of writing (such as 80 words about the student's family, job, country). This will provide examples of the student's ability to form sentences, spell, punctuate, link ideas, use appropriate tenses and vocabulary.

Planning the syllabus

Having ascertained more or less what areas of language need to be covered, the teacher can set about devising a syllabus (what to teach and the order in which to teach it). Even though there might be a balance in favour of, say, social vocabulary, there also usually needs to be variety in lesson types – the four skills, grammar and phonology. By choosing topics carefully, the teacher can incorporate all these into the syllabus. For example, food lexis is presented in one lesson including word stress and pronunciation; in the next lesson, a menu, which includes the food lexis, is used to practise reading skills. Then the same menu is used to practise speaking skills (e.g. ordering food in a restaurant). This sequence also revises and recycles language to help recall.

Memory and recall

Research on memory and recall tells us that regular and systematic revision is essential, otherwise up to 80 per cent of material can be lost over time. The research suggests that the best times to revise and recycle material are: ten minutes after a lesson, 24 hours after a lesson, one week, one month and three months after exposure to material. A practical application of this is to revise the content of a lesson after a ten-minute break, then the next day, at the end of a week, at the end of a month. So, where viable, the teacher can do a quick check on the vocabulary learned in the previous lesson after a short break, then devise a revision test the next day, and so on.

Sample syllabus

Luis is a middle-aged, Spanish businessman at pre-intermediate level. He needs English in order to be able to socialize with clients who he entertains as part of his job. He would like to be able to take them to restaurants and order meals, to make telephone reservations for restaurants, hotels and the theatre and to express his opinion about a performance. His accent is strong, featuring many of the typical characteristics of native speakers of Spanish.

His course lasts one month and comprises three two-hour sessions per week. On the next page is a sample of what could be done in the first week.

	Day One	Day Two	Day Three
1ˢᵗ hour	Needs analysis form 1: teacher with Luis.	Review theatre lexis.	Review functions from Day Two.
	Speaking: 'Something to talk about' cards: teacher makes notes/records. (See Resources and Ideas Bank.)	**Role play:** Phoning to reserve tickets. **Reformulation.** (See Unit 5.)	**Functions:** Restaurant language (e.g. *I'll have, could you/I*).
	Writing: A sample of Luis's written work: 80 words on his job/family, etc.	**Listening:** Student calls theatre information line recorded message. Teacher prepares questions in advance.	**Role play:** Phoning to reserve a table.
	Set a diagnostic test from, e.g. *English Grammar in Use* (Study Guide) for homework.		
2ⁿᵈ hour	**Reading:** Luis skims 3/4 theatre leaflets and chooses a show he'd like to see. Justifies his choice. Teacher prepares questions for scanning task in advance (e.g. phone number, price of tickets, dates).	Repeat role play.	**Listening/lexis:** Booking a hotel room. (*New Headway Pre-Intermediate* Unit 9)
	Lexis: Theatre language, e.g. stalls, interval, box office. Teacher uses Cuisenaire rods to represent parts of the theatre. Luis repeats the lexis.	**Functions:** Expressing dis/pleasure (e.g. *I had a great time; it wasn't bad; I thought it was terrible*).	
	Phonology: Minimal pairs (e.g. /v/ and /b/).	**Phonology:** Minimal pairs (e.g. /ɪ/ and /iː/).	

02

the work space

In this unit you will learn
- about key factors in the immediate one-to-one learning environment

Think about

Which of these seating plans would you consider to be the most conducive to learning?

The teacher of the one-to-one student is likely to teach in one of four places: at school, in her home, in the student's home or at the student's work place. Some students and teachers meet in public places, such as libraries and cafés, though these can be inhibiting and restrict the kinds of activities which can be undertaken.

Seating

If occupying a school room usually used for classes, the teacher needs to spend five minutes or so before the lesson ensuring that the room is tidy and creating a separate work space for the lesson by moving the other chairs to the side. The student will appreciate the fact that this has been done. One thing to bear in mind is whether the student and teacher are left or right-handed. For example, a right-handed teacher is better off sitting to the right of a left-handed student.

The first seating option is student and teacher face to face across the table.

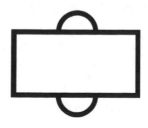

This is reminiscent of interviews and is not conducive to putting the student at ease. If practising interview techniques, however, it is the best way of arranging the seating because it is realistic.

Sitting side by side is more friendly, but perhaps 'friendly' is inappropriate, particularly if the lesson is taking place in the student's office at work.

It can also be uncomfortable, because a certain amount of neck twisting is necessary, but it is the most comfortable position if both are looking at the same sheet.

Another idea is for the teacher and student to sit at right angles to each other.

This works well, being halfway between the formal interview position and the more friendly side by side position. It strikes the right balance for an easy yet professional relationship and is quite comfortable.

It is, of course, appropriate to vary seating arrangements. For example, you might start by sitting at right angles to the student for working on language and then move into a face-to-face position to practise the language and role play. Some role plays, for example customer and shop assistant, are best done standing or, for a restaurant role play, the customer can be sitting and the waitress standing.

Moving away from the table or to another room changes energy levels.

Leaving the room

There are certain activities where the student might prefer to work alone, without being inhibited by the presence of the teacher. For example, the student might find it easier to do written exercises or prepare for role play or a presentation without the teacher. It is important to establish with the student how long he will be left and stick to that time. If working in a school situation, it may be necessary to check school policy here. If it is not permitted, the teacher can simply withdraw to the other side of the room to allow the student space.

Environment

The best kind of light is natural. Ideally, light should come from the left, as the eye and hand move from left to right across the page, which should not be in shadow.

Plants can soften the look of what might otherwise be an austere room.

Many teachers choose to play gentle background music while their students are working. Some find this relaxing; for others it is intrusive. It must be established early on whether or not the student likes background music. Even if music is not played during the lesson itself, having it playing when the student enters the classroom or other work space is welcoming and can even act as an ice breaker.

Lesson length, frequency and breaks

These can be tailor-made to suit the student. In a class, he can alternate between withdrawing and stepping into the limelight, but in a one-to-one situation, may feel the pressure of being the only student and need shorter lessons or more breaks.

03 listening to the student

In this unit you will learn
- about aspects of listening actively to your student
- about the use of silence and waiting time

Think about

Which of these behaviours are indicative of good listening?

a looking around the room while the student is talking
b allowing the student to sit in silence to collect his thoughts
c finishing the student's sentences
d encouraging the student to talk in his own words without fear of mistakes or correction
e butting in with your own opinions and experiences
f using elicitation devices like *Tell me about* ...
g echoing what the student says as a habitual response
h simply acknowledging what the student has said, whether *content* ('Really? Mmm') or *language* ('Good')

Listening

A language teacher needs to be a superlative listener and in the one-to-one scenario this ability is of great importance.

Clearly **a, c, e** and **g** above are strategies indicative of ineffective listening and attention, while the others show ways of promoting and valuing student talk.

Think about

How long do you wait on average between asking a student a question and waiting for a response?

a 5 seconds   c 30 seconds
b 20 seconds   d 45 seconds

Silence and waiting time

Silence and the handling of it can be a challenge when interacting with any individual. When spending time with a student for fixed time spans where we cannot simply excuse ourselves and walk off, the approach to silence needs some thought. Silences can be seen as spaces to be filled but also as positive processing and digestion periods.

It may be very difficult for a student to think constructively when there is a lot of 'noise', i.e. teacher talk and alongside that pressure from the teacher for the student to produce language or talk on demand. When the teacher asks a question or provides a prompt to elicit language or talk, the student first has to process it, then decide on the content of what he is going to say, and then encode it in an unfamiliar language. That takes time, especially at low levels and for students whose first language is very different from English. For example, the Thai language is much further removed from English than French in terms of its grammar and vocabulary.

It can be rewarding for the teacher to experiment with waiting time when eliciting language or information. Many teachers find that prolonging the time they allow students to think and respond by a factor of 3–4 times can be very productive even though it feels awkward at first. The awkwardness may often be within the teacher rather than the student, who probably has all his faculties and available attention involved in processing language, thoughts, and feelings. Experience shows that when teachers significantly increase their tolerance of silence and prolong waiting time, the student increases in his willingness to speak and in the amount of contribution he makes.

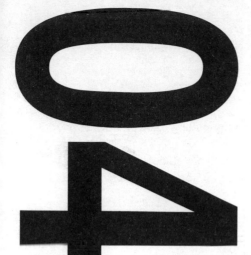

04

learner styles

In this unit you will learn
- about individual learner differences
- how to identify and cater for your student's preferred learning style

Think about

When you are learning a word in a new language, do you need to:

a see it soon?
b write it down soon?
c hear it soon?
d say it soon?

If you need to do all of these, try putting them in order of priority for you.

• Which of these would you get your student to do first?
• What do you think this tells you about your learning style, the way you learn a language?

Research on language learners suggests that students vary enormously in the way they prefer to learn and the way they actually learn. The danger for teachers is that they might tend to teach students in the way that they learn themselves. This disadvantages students who learn very differently from their teacher. It is worth becoming aware of the major differences in the way that students approach their learning and, where possible, to take these into account when teaching. Clearly this can be complex while teaching a group. With only one student, the teacher has the opportunity to tune in to a particular learner's preferences.

Background: Mind and body

There are a number of schools of thought, both eastern and western, ancient and modern, which see the mind and body as the mind-body. This perspective suggests that any activity in the mind is reflected in a corresponding activity in the body and vice versa. For example, the common states of consciousness, waking, dreaming and sleeping each have a corresponding state of the neurophysiology. In the dreaming state there will be a specific style of functioning in the body – metabolic rate, brainwave activity – corresponding to that mental state. It is possible, therefore, for a scientist to tell whether someone is awake, dreaming, or sleeping – their *mental* state – simply by monitoring their brain activity – their *physical* state. By extension it might be possible to tell what kind of language learner your student is simply by monitoring what kind of language his body speaks.

Rudolf Steiner

Rudolf Steiner (1861–1925) was an Austrian educator and the founder of Anthroposophy – a philosophy which envisions people as complete and whole spiritual beings. Steiner incorporated the idea of identifying learner styles and ensuring they were catered for into his system of education.

Steiner classified his pupils using the medieval system of humours, seeing them as *sanguine* (the carefree, lively child), *choleric* (the strong, masterful type), *melancholic* (quiet and sensitive), or *phlegmatic* (the student who is easy-going and inclined to laziness). The teacher organizes the classroom into four groups, seating each pupil with like-body-minded types. Lessons are then taught from four different angles to make them accessible to each mind-body type.

Ayurveda

Ayurveda is the holistic health care system of ancient India. Ayurveda makes a highly systematic and detailed correlation between an individual's physiology, behavioural tendencies, and mental functioning. The system makes a tripartite classification of mind-body types – *vata*, *pitta* and *kapha*. If you have a light build, and an aversion to cold weather, you may have a *vata* constitution and be quick to learn and quick to forget. A *pitta* type will have a medium frame, an aversion to hot weather and have a good general memory. A *kapha* person will have a large build, an aversion to damp, cool weather and have a good long-term memory. On the next page is a simplified guide to the three types.

Ayurveda calls the three types *dosas*. The majority of people have one dominant *dosa* and a secondary *dosa*. For example, a *vata-pitta* person, while being thin in build, quick-moving and talkative, would typically benefit from the more enterprising nature and stronger digestion of *pitta* and have more tolerance of cold. From the outline below you may begin to be able to discern your own mind-body type and that of your student. The relevance here is to be aware how differently people learn and function. The points on mental activity and memory are of course particularly relevant to learning and teaching.

If your student is primarily a *vata* type, then he will pick up vocabulary quickly but also forget it very quickly. It will be very important to do regular ongoing revision of everything that you

	vata	*pitta*	*kapha*
Hair	dry	fine, thinning	thick, oily
Skin	dry, rough	soft, ruddy	oily, moist
Weather	aversion to cold	aversion to heat	aversion to damp, cool weather
Sleep	interrupted, light	sound, medium length	sound, long, heavy
Reaction to stress	excites easily, anxious	angers easily, critical	not easily ruffled, stubborn
Body size	small frame	medium frame	gains weight easily
Hunger	irregular	sharp	can easily skip meals
Walk	quick	determined	slow and steady
Moods	change quickly	intense, slowly changing	steady, non-changing
Mental activity	quick and restless, imaginative	sharp intellect, efficient, perfectionist	calm, steady, stable, methodical
Memory	quick to learn, quick to forget	good general memory	good long-term memory, slow to grasp new information

teach such a learner. It will also be important to build plenty of variety into a learning session to engage the restless *vata* mind. Any activity requiring imagination will be relevant and effective.

Your *pitta* student will be keen on accuracy and getting everything right and may get annoyed with himself easily.

The *kapha* student will have good stamina and undertake activities in a steady and calm manner.

Becoming aware of these mind-body characteristics will keep you alert to your student's needs and enable you to empathize and attune yourself to his style of working. Even noticing that *vata* feels the cold, *pitta* the heat, and *kapha* is averse to cold and damp may be relevant to understanding how they are feeling in different weather conditions and ensuring that the temperature in the study room is appropriate.

Three trainees on a teacher training course epitomized the three *dosas* in the way they coped:

• Nick, an Australian, showed *pitta* characteristics – fine, red hair and a medium build, he was enthusiastic, sharp and enterprising. He was very critical of his performance in teaching practice and aimed for perfection.

• Maria, an Italian, was an archetypal *vata*. She was slim with quick movements, prone to incessant worry and insomnia

during the course. She was imaginative and lively as a teacher.
• Caroline, British, had a *kapha* build. She was imperturbable and showed good stamina. She needed time to absorb new material.

Being alert to their different styles and approaches to the course enabled me to be non-judgemental and understand the challenges each faced.

NLP

A less intricate and maybe more accessible approach to identifying learner style is offered by one particular aspect of Neuro-Linguistic Programming (NLP).

Neuro-Linguistic Programming is a body of knowledge developed in the 1970s by John Grinder, then Assistant Professor of Linguistics, and Richard Bandler, a psychology student, both at the University of California, Santa Cruz.

NLP deals with the structure of human, subjective experience, how we organize what we see, hear, and feel, how we describe that in language and how we act both consciously and unconsciously to achieve results.

Eyes, ears, and heart

The particular insight of NLP which is of immediate practical value to language teachers is the way in which learners can be identified as predominantly *visual*, *auditory*, or *kinaesthetic*.

Visual learners take in information through the eyes; they prefer to see language written down, read it, look at pictures and diagrams; they take notes to refer to again later. *Auditory* learners prefer to receive information through the ears; they like to hear language spoken, listen to tapes, repeat words to themselves aloud or subvocally. *Kinaesthetic* learners prefer to access information through their hands or bodies or emotions; they like to touch things, move, walk around; they take notes because the physical response of writing helps them to absorb information.

As in Ayurveda, where an individual commonly has one dominant *dosa* and a secondary less dominant *dosa*, for example, *kapha-pitta*, a learner may be, for example, *visual kinaesthetic* or *auditory visual*.

	visual	*auditory*	*kinaesthetic*
Recall	remembers what was seen	remembers what was discussed, i.e. heard and said	has an overall impression of what was experienced
Conversation	needs the whole picture, very detailed	talkative, loves discussions and may monopolize, likes red herrings, will tell a whole sequence	laconic, tactile gesture and movements, uses action words
Spelling	accurate, sees words, is only confused when words are new	phonetic, spells with rhythmic movement	counts out letters with movements, checks with internal feelings
Reading	excellent and fast, would rather read than be read to	enjoys reading aloud, reads slowly because subvocalizes a lot	likes books with a strong plot, reflects the action of the text with body movements
Writing	neatness is important	talks better than he writes, likes to talk while writing	thick, pressured handwriting
Imagination	vivid images, sees possibilities, details, good at long-term plans	hears sounds and voices	acts an image out – wants to 'walk through it'
Learning	needs an overview, cautious until everything is clear in his head, memorizes in pictures	dialogues internally and externally, tries alternatives orally first; memorizes by steps, procedure, sequence; easily distracted	learns through touching and doing
Voice	chin up, high voice	agile in shifting pitch and tempo	chin down, voice deep and loud

(from *Ways of Doing* by Davis, Garside, Rinvolucri – Cambridge University Press, 1999)

Main characteristics

On page 22 is a summary of some main characteristics of each learner type taken from *Righting the educational conveyor belt* by John Grinder (Metamorphous Press, 1991), the co-founder of NLP.

Eye movement

An immediate route to identifying the dominant sense is through monitoring eye movement – a very observable element of body language. Again, the activity of the body reflects the activity on the mental level. Here is the system for a right-handed person:

If a student looks up when he is thinking, this indicates he is accessing or representing information **visually**.

- If asked what the word for something is, he will be seeing it internally: if he looks up and to the right, this indicates he is *constructing* a visual image; if he looks up and to the left, he is *recalling* a whole visual image. He may of course switch between the two modes, alternately recalling and constructing visually.

If the student looks to either side in the direction of his ears, he is accessing or representing information **auditorily**.

- If asked for a word, he will be hearing it internally: if he looks to the right, he will be *constructing* an auditory image; if he looks to the left, he will be *recalling* it.

If the student looks down, he will be accessing information **kinaesthetically**.

- If asked for a word, he will be feeling it internally: if he looks down to the left, he may be talking to himself, subvocalizing.

The pattern of constructing versus recalling information is reversed in a left-handed person.

Diagnosis

One way of becoming familiar with this system is to carry out a simple activity with volunteers. Draw up a list of, say, six questions – two for each sense. For example:

1 What does your front door look like?
2 What did your very first school look like when you were a child?
3 Think about a piece of music you like – what do the first few seconds sound like?
4 What's your best friend's voice like?
5 You're sitting on an aeroplane. What does it feel like?
6 What does a cat's fur feel like?

Sit opposite your volunteer. Find out if they are left or right handed and ask the questions. Tell them not to answer aloud but to simply think about the answers. Notice their eye movements in response to each question. Depending on whether the eyes move to the left or right, you may notice to what extent they are able to recall information clearly, need to build it up, invent it or use a combination of these. You may need to ask further questions before a pattern of dominance of one sensory channel emerges. It is interesting to take them back through the questions asking them again and then finding out what their internal experiences were for each question. For example, in response to the question about a piece of music, they may have seen the musician or the CD cover (eyes up), they may have heard the instruments playing (eyes to the side), they may have had an emotional response (eyes down), or a combination of two or all of these in a particular sequence.

Your student

When working with your student, you can simply notice how his eyes move when he is thinking. You can also carry out the same experiment above, asking him a series of questions without requiring an oral response. You can then discuss his preferred channel and learning style. One way of incorporating the experiment into a lesson is to ask questions about a particular topic area that you are covering.

For example, if you are teaching vocabulary connected to food, then all of the questions can be food related – you are sitting in a very nice restaurant, look around, what is it like? What can you hear? You are eating soup – what do you notice? What can you smell? and so on. The first time the student thinks about the answers, the second time he responds orally. In this way he need not even know what you are up to! This provides a sound procedure for oral production with in-built time to think.

Dictation idea

A related lesson activity is to take a set of vocabulary you have already taught. Dictate the items, whether individual words or phrases, to the student and he sorts each word or phrase into one of three columns based on whether he sees, hears, or feels the item.

I see	I hear	I feel

The student should write the words in the column that seems right quickly and without too much thought. Then ask the student to explain why he put each word where he did. Another way of using dictation is as a way into a reading or listening activity. Dictate key words from the text or tape for the student to categorize. You can then also ask the student to make predictions about the text/tape. Write these predictions down and the first reading/listening task can be to check which are right and wrong.

Lesson applications

Let's take a look at a few example activities and tasks which give a flavour of what may be relevant to the three learner types. These are probably techniques with which you are already familiar but it is worth revisiting them from the point of view of the three learner types. It may be that if, for example, you are a visual learner, then you will tend to favour visually oriented activities. This may be creating obstacles for students who learn very differently. It may also be worth using techniques appropriate to all three learner types to balance activities and energies for the student. This would be advisable when teaching two or more learners, in order to cater for everyone.

Vocabulary

1 Visual learner
The learner needs to work with seeing the vocabulary.

- Match words to visuals or definitions.
- Show the student a list of words and ask which word means x, e.g. a place where you borrow books.
- Point to a word and the student pronounces it.
- The student matches word parts:

2 Auditory learner
The student needs to work with hearing the words spoken by another or by himself.

- Elicit/present and drill vocabulary, e.g. What do we call the place where you go to borrow books?
- Give a clear auditory model with a pause before asking the student to repeat.
- Have a list of words numbered, say a word and the student gives the number or say a number and the student says the word.

3 Kinaesthetic learner

The student needs to work with responding physically or emotionally to the words.

- Show a list of words and give a definition; the student points to the word. This can be done by more and more rapidly recycling the definitions and words to maintain focus and pace.
- Have the words on cards, give the meaning and the student picks up the card with the correct word.
- Turn the cards face down, one card is turned face up for a few seconds and then returned face down, the student writes the word down (see Unit 8, Cards and Reusable Laminated Cards for more ideas of this type).
- As revision of vocabulary, dictate words to the student.
- As revision or to allow the student to grasp spelling, draw a word in the air; the student reads it.
- The student sorts words into those he loves, does or doesn't like. This can be the basis for a dictation activity:

I love	I like	I don't like

This can be a revision activity and draws on the kinaesthetic learner's inclination to relate to language on the level of feeling.

Phonology

1 Visual learner

The student needs to work with seeing how language items are pronounced.

- Mouth a word from a short list and the student identifies it (exaggerate the mouth shape). Then the student mouths a word for you to identify. This is effective with minimal pairs where the difference between the pair is visible, e.g. *ship* and *sheep* where the lips are spread for the second word.

- Show the mouth shape and get the student to make the shape using a mirror to check.

- Mark stress on words.
  - ■
  - basket

- Mark stress on phrases and sentences.

  ■   ■
  fish and *chips*

            ■   ■
  Could you *pass* me the *sugar*?
- Use arrows to show intonation.

  ↗   ↘
  Pardon?   Which one?
- Bracket silent syllables: *comf* [*or*]*table.*
- Use Cuisenaire rods for features of phonology (see Unit 7, Cuisenaire Rods).

2 Auditory learner

The student needs to work with getting a clear acoustic image of the way language sounds.

- Give an uncluttered model of pronunciation – *pause*, then model the item, then *pause* before asking the student to repeat. The second pause allows the student time to process and recreate the sounds internally.
- When doing minimal pairs work, cover your mouth so that the student focuses purely on the sounds without any visual input. Ask the student which sound or word you are producing from a list, e.g. *leap* or *lip*?

3 Kinaesthetic learner

The student needs to work on responding physically or getting a feel for the way language is pronounced.

- Have a list of words with different stress patterns, beat or tap a word for the student to identify; you can begin with just two words (e.g. *Paris, Peru*), then gradually add one word at a time (e.g. *Panama*) as the student becomes more confident.
- Use an elastic band to show how stressed syllables are longer than unstressed syllables. Start with two words, use the elastic band to illustrate the stress pattern, e.g. stretch the band for the first syllable of *Paris* and release it for the second syllable. Exaggerated stretching works best to highlight syllable length, just as with an auditory student exaggeration of the volume of the stressed syllable highlights it. Ask the student to identify the word you showed. Then add further words.
- Use Cuisenaire rods for features of phonology (see Unit 7, Cuisenaire Rods).

Reading

1 Visual learner
The student will enjoy visualizing scenes and characters.

- Ask questions such as: *What do you think the writer/character looks like?* With reference to a conversation ask: *Where do you think they are? Can you describe the place?*
- Ask the student to draw a scene described or a character – Cuisenaire rods can be used here instead (see Unit 7, Cuisenaire Rods).

2 Auditory learner
The student will enjoy relating to sounds and voices.

- Ask questions such as: *What kind of voice do you think he/she has?*
- In a descriptive passage ask: *What sounds/noises do you think there are?*
- Read out a text which you have already worked on and pause for the student to fill in missing words. With a short text this can be done several times, omitting different items each time.

3 Kinaesthetic learner
The student will enjoy responding to movement, mood and feelings.

- Ask questions such as: *How do you think the character feels? What mood is he/she in? How do you think he/she sits/walks?*

Listening

1 Visual learner
- Ask questions about a taped passage such as: *What do you think the speaker looks like? Where do you think she is? What's she wearing? Is she sitting/standing/walking? Is she inside/outside?*
- Use a transcript – this can be gapped, need the sentences putting in the right order or include deliberate mistakes.

2 Auditory learner
- As a tuning-in exercise, you can get the student to focus on sounds and voices. Ask questions such as: *How many speakers are there? What age do you think they are? What*

sounds can you hear in the background? With a song you can ask: *How many singers are there? What instruments can you hear?*

3 Kinaesthetic learner

• You can focus on mood and character.
• You can use physical response activities – have key words on cards; the student points to or picks up the card when the word is spoken. Write down the names/roles of the speakers, the student points to the name/role when they are speaking. The student can raise his hand when certain words are mentioned.

Conclusion

Clearly, no learner can be reduced to a single type, whether *sanguine, vata pitta* or *kinaesthetic visual.* It might be more useful to notice how the tendencies and the main characteristics outlined in this chapter are each expressed in learners in different ways, proportions and combinations. Every learner is in some or many ways different from every other learner; it is worth becoming aware at least of ways of exploring what works best with each one-to-one student. Above all, you need to remember that what works best for you might not work best for your student.

reformulation

In this unit you will learn
- about the concept of reformulation
- how to use techniques of reformulation, paraphrase and summary to improve your student's accuracy and expressiveness

Think about

What value could there be in repeating a student's sentences in a correct or more sophisticated form?

Background

Reformulation is a technique derived from counselling. It is also used as a primary procedure in a method based on counselling – Community Language Learning, which is a method of language learning developed in the 1970s by Charles Curran, a professor of psychology at Loyola University in Chicago.

There are parallels between counselling and Community Language Learning: in conventional counselling the client articulates his problem and the counsellor *reformulate*s (reflects back, paraphrases, or summarizes) the issue.

Part of the process of reflecting back is of value in showing the client that he has been heard when he may not have been truly 'heard' or valued before. Paraphrasing demonstrates that the client has been heard and can be a way of prompting him to move on. Summarizing involves picking up on the main feelings and themes.

In Community Language Learning the student says what he wants to say in his first language, for example, Japanese, and the teacher *reformulates* or, in this case, translates what he has said into the target language, English. This has a potentially therapeutic and nourishing value in that the student knows and feels the teacher is attending to him. It also provides an accurate target language version of what the student wants to say as close as possible to his level of English.

Community Language Learning was originally designed for monolingual classes where the teacher is a speaker of both the students' first language and the target language. The students sit in a circle around a cassette recorder. A student addresses another learner in the group in his own language. For example, a German speaker might ask another student in the group: *Wie geht's?* The teacher translates, providing the English version. For example, the teacher translates this as: *How are you?* When the student has heard and repeated the English sentence and/or is confident about reproducing it, he records it on to the tape. The lesson continues in this way, with students being given the

English translation of what they want to say to each other by the teacher. This is all recorded on the tape until a conversation entirely in English is built up. The tape can then be played and some or all of the language transcribed for further work. Where translation is not an option, the student produces an utterance in English and the teacher reformulates it. If the utterance is entirely correct and appropriate, the teacher may simply repeat it. If it is inappropriate in some way, the teacher reformulates it, remaining as close as possible to the original message.

With this approach, it is the student who decides what he wants to say. The teacher provides a *reformulation* in the form of a translation at a level of language which is close to or just above the competence of the learner. The syllabus and language content is entirely student driven. Reformulation is very appropriate in one-to-one teaching, where the language area can be decided by what the student wants or needs to say.

Modes of reformulation

Translation

When the teacher speaks the student's first language, the original Community Language Learning model can be used. The student says what he wants to say in his own language and the teacher reformulates his sentence in English. The contribution of the teacher here is to choose the language exponents which stay as close to the student's message as possible and at the same time can be managed by the student at his level.

Reformulation from English to English

At post-beginner levels and where the teacher does not speak the student's first language, the student produces an English sentence and if it is correct, the teacher can simply repeat it. The reformulation acts as confirmation of correctness and provides exposure to a reliable phonological model.

Student	*I'm an engineer.*
Teacher	*I'm an engineer.*

An alternative reformulation here is for the teacher to reflect back in the 'you' form/second person.

Student	*I'm an engineer.*
Teacher	*You're an engineer.*

Correction

When the student makes a mistake, the teacher reformulates the utterance in the correct form.

Student   *I can to swim.*
Teacher   *I can swim./You can swim.*

Paraphrase

The teacher can reformulate or paraphrase the student's utterance with greater linguistic sophistication in order to extend the learner's range.

Student   *Tokyo is a very, very big city.*
Teacher   *So, Tokyo is an enormous city.*
Student   *I live in Bangkok. It is the main city in Thailand.*
Teacher   *So, you live in Bangkok, which is the capital of Thailand.*

Formality

The teacher can also reformulate more formally as appropriate. Here the paraphrase is from informal to more formal.

Student   *Where's the loo?*
Teacher   *Can you tell me where the toilet is, please?*

Here the reformulation is from inappropriate abruptness to polite request:

Student   *Give me one beer.*
Teacher   *Can I have a beer, please?*

Sentence or sentences

The following procedures are led by the student's input and work on accuracy and building up a repertoire of chunks for the student. These are especially appropriate at lower levels, where the student's own language may be limited and a lot of support, consolidation and security is provided. These approaches are also very useful for a student of any level who is concerned about accuracy at whatever stage of his learning.

A learner who is less concerned with accuracy and more with fluency and getting his message across may find these techniques wearisome, frustrating and irrelevant. Such a student may respond better to an oral or written summary approach. When followed orally, as in the examples below, these procedures may favour an auditory learner. A visual or kinaesthetic learner may benefit from written reformulation at some stage (see Unit 4, Learner Styles).

Procedure A   One procedure is for the student and teacher to work sentence by sentence, with reformulation by the teacher. In the examples, the topic chosen by the student is a job he once had.

Student	*I worked in an office during three years.*
Teacher	*I worked in an office for three years.*
Student	*It was very good job.*
Teacher	*It was a very good job.*
Student	*I much.*
Teacher	*I learned a lot.*

At the end of the sequence, the student can summarize what he has said and this can be recorded. The teacher could then reformulate the student's summary and record it. The student now has his own version and the teacher's version to compare and listen to at home.

Procedure B   Another option is for the student to repeat the teacher's reformulation at each step to consolidate accuracy.

Student	*I worked in an office during three years.*
Teacher	*I worked in an office for three years. Repeat* (or a gesture).
Student	*I worked in an office for three years … It was very good job.*
Teacher	*It was a very good job. Repeat* (or a gesture).
Student	*It was a very good job … I learned much.*
Teacher	*I learned a lot. Repeat* (or a gesture).
Student	*I learned a lot.*

An option here is to record each line spoken by the student after he has repeated the teacher's reformulation to his satisfaction. In this way, a whole talk by the student is built up line by line on the tape. Once the cassette player has been set to record, the pause button can be used to stop and start the tape to record each sentence. This would follow the model proposed by Community Language Learning. The final recorded version could then be transcribed by the student for homework, with later teacher verification. Alternatively the teacher could replay the tape line by line for the student to transcribe. Or the student could replay the tape line by line for the teacher to transcribe.

Another option is for the student to summarize everything he has said without interruption. This provides more practice and, with the repetition of the task, it may be that the student's English is more accurate and sophisticated. Now that he is clear about his message and exactly what he is going to say, the learner can pay more attention to form. The teacher can then summarize the student's summary, exposing the student to a full, correct, and fully comprehensible version of his account. Again, the most recent summaries by the student and by the teacher can be recorded.

Procedure C   A further option is for the student to summarize everything he has said after each teacher reformulation. The teacher then feeds back the summary.

Student	*I worked in an office during three years.*
Teacher	*I worked in an office for three years. Repeat* (or a gesture).
Student	*I worked in an office for three years... It was very good job.*
Teacher	*I worked in an office for three years. It was a very good job. Repeat* (or a gesture).
Student	*I worked in an office for three years. It was a very good job... I learned much.*
Teacher	*I worked in an office for three years. It was a very good job. I learned a lot. Repeat* (or gesture).
Student	*I worked in an office for three years. It was a very good job. I learned a lot ... .*

Recordings can now be made by the student and then the teacher.

Summarizing

The student speaks at length about his job. The teacher listens with full attention and, when the student has finished or at an appropriate point, summarizes what the student said. The student can then summarize the teacher's summary. This builds in the benefit of task repetition. At first the student's attention will have been engaged in content, in his message. With the opportunity to repeat the task, there is the possibility of increased accuracy and sophistication when more of the learner's attention is available to focus on form. Further chances to repeat the task can be offered, with the student working to summarize what he said against the clock with a time limit and even ever-shortening time limits. This provides an element of challenge if the repetition of the same task appears tedious. Finally, a recorded version can be made by the student and the teacher.

Summarizing content and feeling

When reformulating a student's speech, the teacher can reflect on how the student seems to be feeling about the content. Clearly, this requires greater attentiveness on the teacher's part. In the example, her reflections on feelings are underlined.

Teacher   *So, you worked in an office for three years, <u>which you seemed to find very valuable</u> as you learned a lot. <u>I think you enjoyed the job a lot</u>.*

The teacher may want to check her interpretations with the student.

Teacher   *So, you worked in an office for three years, <u>which you seemed to find very valuable</u> as you learned a lot. Is that right? … <u>I think you enjoyed the job a lot. Is that right?</u>*

Written reformulation of speech

The student talks at length on a topic, e.g. My best holiday. The teacher listens attentively without interruption. The student is then asked to start again from the beginning of his talk and the teacher writes down what the student says as he goes along so that he can watch his language being reformulated in writing by the teacher. This may have the effect of getting the student to pay more attention to form and accuracy. The student now has a written record of his reformulated talk. This can then be recorded by the teacher and then by the student for further consolidation and a spoken record.

A variation on this procedure is to record the student giving his talk and then to replay it in segments and reformulate the segments orally for the student to write down as a dictation. Finally check the student's dictation.

Written reformulation of written text

The student is given a task to complete in writing. This could be a written version of a spoken task. The teacher introduces the task, for example, *Let's have a conversation*. The task is then carried out in silence. So the teacher and student have a conversation on paper. The teacher might begin by writing:

How are you?

The student replies:

Very fine.

Underneath this, and in brackets to signal a reformulation, the teacher writes:

(Fine, thanks.)

If what the student writes is in no need of reformulation, the teacher simply ticks it. For example, the student writes:

How was your weekend? (✔)

When the task is complete, the written conversation can be rehearsed and then recorded. This provides the student with a written and recorded version of the task. This is a useful way of rehearsing speech and potential dialogues. Use can be made of the needs analysis in which the learner has specified the potential speakers he needs to engage in conversation. Role plays can be enacted on paper in this way as a precursor to spoken roleplaying. A further option is for the student to play both parts of a role play, with the teacher reformulating both parts on paper. This process provides a strong security factor for students who need their confidence building before engaging in a spoken role play.

The same procedure can be adopted with a written task: for example, the student writes a letter of invitation, a message, instructions, directions, a story or an essay. After each sentence the teacher writes in a reformulation in brackets or simply adds a tick. Alternatively, the student is asked to write the complete text and the teacher reformulates it on a separate sheet. The teacher could do this after the lesson, to be given back next time or while the student is involved in another task.

Spoken reformulation of written text

The student completes a written task, such as drafting a letter of complaint. The teacher reads the letter and records it on to tape, reformulating as necessary. The teacher then adds recorded comments on spelling and punctuation at the end. The student takes the tape home and uses it to rewrite and improve on the first draft. (See Unit 9, Corresponding and Writing, for more detail on this procedure.)

Student reformulating teacher

Another option is for the teacher to talk about a topic and for the student to listen carefully and finally summarize orally what was said. This can also be a way of exemplifying a student task. For example, the teacher begins a session by talking about what she did the previous weekend. The student listens and summarizes – *So, you ...* This is followed by the student recounting his weekend and the teacher providing a summary.

The Resources and Ideas Bank (page 167) provides a list of topics which can be used for students to speak on for reformulation work. Good use can also be made here of the needs analysis – the student can work through the topics he has targeted.

06

coursebooks, retrospective coursebooks and blank tapes

In this unit you will learn
- how to adapt published material
- how to create a personalized coursebook with your student
- about the value of recording your student

Think about

How might the recording of a gap-fill exercise on to tape be beneficial to the student outside the classroom?

Prospective/retrospective coursebooks

It frequently happens that a coursebook is used prospectively, i.e. teacher and student use it as a pre-ordained syllabus to work through. There is, of course, a place for conventional coursebook use in one-to-one teaching.

A conventional coursebook can be dipped into to meet a student's needs, whether it is using the grammar section, a pronunciation exercise or topic-linked skills work. Meanwhile, a retrospective coursebook can evolve in tandem to include texts and material chosen by the student and teacher, records and summaries of language met, and reformulated work. As a syllabus, this grows out of the process of work done – especially that involving reformulation (see Unit 5, Reformulation). In this way, the retrospective coursebook acts as a record of the course. The teacher can keep a copy in case the student returns for a further course.

Tape

Like any coursebook, the retrospective coursebook has an accompanying tape or tapes. The tapes, however, are not pre-recorded but consist of recordings made by both the teacher and the student throughout the developing course. They will consist of:

> reformulations,
> recordings of oral work,
> recorded versions of written scripts completed by the student,
> recordings of reading texts,
> recordings of written tasks and language exercises completed during lessons.

The tapes, too, become a record of the course – an aural record of almost everything done to complement the personalized coursebook. It is worth considering making some kind of taped version of every activity completed in lessons. Together, the book and tapes provide a permanent reference for revision and consolidation.

Organizing the retrospective coursebook

The retrospective coursebook provides a course record. The student can organize it in a looseleaf file under the following headings: vocabulary, grammar, skills, phonology.

Organizing vocabulary

By topic   One way of organizing vocabulary is to list it under topic headings, e.g. sport, crime, food, and to organize the topics alphabetically. The words recorded under one topic heading may have come from different lessons. Vocabulary in subsequent lessons can be added to the original list. Here is an example of a vocabulary page organized by topic:

Alphabetically   Another method of recording vocabulary is to do so alphabetically, although the lack of connections between words could be unhelpful. The student could buy an address book and use the A to Z system to organize lexis.

Whatever system is used for organizing the vocabulary the student could write a definition – preferably in English, and with a translation if he wishes – alongside the word/phrase. Some words, of

Music
Types of music
■ *classical*
rock
People
■ *musician*
■ *singer*
guitarist
Instruments
■ *guitar*
■ *saxophone*
drum
■ *drumsticks*

course, are not easily translated, so putting words into written contexts can be very helpful for future reference. This is especially true in the case of 'false friends'.

Where pronunciation is a problem, phonemic script can be used. Stress can also be marked. Here, for example, is an entry by a French-speaking student:

word/expression	part of speech	meaning	example sentence
■ worry	verb	s'inquiéter	Don't worry about your exam. It'll be OK.

There could be a separate page in the vocabulary section for collocations, which the student can add to whenever he comes across relevant words. For example, collocations can be organized by key word, e.g. *do, make,* or *home*:

do my homework   *make a sandwich*   *home from home*
do an exam   *make the bed*   *home in on*

Organizing grammar

This can be organized in the file alphabetically according to area, e.g. gerunds, prepositions of time, present perfect.

Organizing skills

This section can be organized under *reading, writing, listening* and *speaking*. An alternative approach for skills work would be to organize it where relevant by topic or theme. For example, reading, writing, listening, and speaking material all linked to the food topic could be filed under **food**.

Organizing phonology

This could be one simple heading or subdivided into sounds, word stress, sentence stress, connected speech, intonation.

The blank tape

Diagnosis

Initially, the tape can help the teacher with assessing student needs and designing the syllabus. Having recorded the student speaking, the teacher can replay the tape for diagnostic purposes.

During and after lessons

During the course, the student can use the tape both in lessons and for homework if he has access to a tape recorder. An easy homework task which provides exposure to the language is for the student to listen to a recording just before going to sleep and/or on waking. There is a school of thought which says that the brain is especially receptive to information during the 'twilight' period between waking and sleeping. The tape can also be listened to in the car or on a personal stereo.

Students and tapes

Students are often nervous about the idea of recording, perhaps never having heard themselves speaking English before. Interestingly, they tend to perform better for a tape, knowing that they are going public and that what they say will be on record. It is important that the student does not feel uncomfortable about being recorded, though it may take a little while before he is entirely comfortable with listening to himself. If the student has control of the record button, he can begin when he is ready. Furthermore, knowing he will have the opportunity to listen to the recording and improve on his performance (see Unit 5, Reformulation) is also motivating and reassuring.

Using the tape

In practice, more than one blank tape will probably be in use. In fact it might be worth organizing the recordings on to several tapes, one for each of the following:

- language exercises
- reformulated work
- teacher recordings
- phonology work

Language exercises

Language exercises can be set on tape for homework or they can be recorded with the answers as part of a lesson to provide a record of the exercise for the student to take away and review. This may benefit the auditory learner (see Unit 4, Learner Styles), who can listen to exercises in the car, at home or on a personal stereo. Making a taped version during the lesson after the exercise has been completed will also prevent the student from gobbling material too quickly.

Gap-fills

For example:

They live ___ the coast. (Answer: *on*)

There are several ways in which the tape can be used in conjunction with such a gap-filling task.

- The teacher reads the entire exercise, including the answers and the student takes it away to listen to in his own time. The gap-fill is then completed on paper in the next lesson.
- The gap-fill is carried out in the lesson in the usual way and the teacher then records it with the answers for the student to take away to listen to as a review.
- The teacher reads the sentences of the exercise, pausing her voice (not the tape) at a gap. After a few seconds, the teacher records the language missing from the gap. The student takes the tape away for homework. This gives the student time to think about the answer before having it confirmed by the teacher. Replaying it will help to reinforce those answers. Repeating the task results in the student recalling the answers as part of a complete text and helps the memorization of chunks of language. The gap-fill can be completed on paper in the usual way in a subsequent lesson.
- The teacher reads the sentences, pausing her voice (not the tape) when she reaches a gap. After a few seconds, the teacher continues the sentence, without recording the missing language. Again, the student supplies the answer but, this time, he does not have confirmation from the teacher. The student can write his answers for correction in the next lesson.

Multiple choice

For example:

They live (**a**) *on   the coast.* (Answer: *on*)
       (**b**) *in*
       (**c**) *at*
       (**d**) *with*

Similar approaches to those adopted for gap-fills can be used here.

- The teacher records the whole exercise including each of the multiple choices. The correct choice is then added after a pause for thought.
- The whole exercise is recorded for homework without the correct answer being given.
- The multiple choice exercise is carried out in the usual way in the lesson and then a recording is made there and then with the answers included for the student to take away.

Transformation exercises

For example:

> *The last time I saw her was two weeks ago.*
> *I haven't* _____
> (Answer: *seen her for two weeks*)

Again, a similar approach can be used.

- The exercise can be recorded including the unfinished sentence, with a pause left for the answer. Optionally, the answer can be recorded after the pause. This can be given for homework and gone over in the lesson.

- The exercise can be completed in the usual way in a lesson and a taped version made there and then once the correct answers have been established. The teacher can record the exercise and the student can record the answer.

Questions

The teacher can record a set of questions, leaving spaces on the tape for the student to rehearse or even record his answers. These could be questions in an interview style asking for personal information:

> *How often do you watch television?*
> *What are your favourite programmes?*
> *Do you watch the advertisements?* etc.

Questions can be couched in a particular verb form or include a grammatical point, for example, the present perfect and the superlative:

> *What's the worst film you've ever seen?*
> *What's the cheapest holiday you've ever had?*

The opportunity to listen to the teacher's questions and prepare answers in advance allows rehearsal time, which, for a student who is reluctant to speak, could be extremely reassuring.

Listen and repeat

Recording lends itself very well to focusing on the phonological aspects of language. The teacher can record herself with the student repeating what she says. The student can then take the recording away and compare his speech with the teacher's, paying attention to the particular aspect of phonology which is being practised – whether it is intonation, specific sounds, word or sentence stress. The exercise can be repeated after an interval of, for example, two weeks, so that the two versions can be compared and progress noted.

Role play

The teacher can record one half of a dialogue for the student to take home and listen to with a view to preparing his own part. This gives the student plenty of thinking and preparation time. The role play is then carried out in the next lesson. It can be repeated, with the teacher and student swapping roles a few times. Finally, the role play is recorded with the teacher and student taking it in turns to play each role. The student can take the tape home as a review.

Here is an example of what the teacher could record for a role play of a car accident involving a police officer and an eye-witness.

Where were you when you saw the accident?

_____

Can you describe the vehicle?

_____

How fast do you think it was going?

_____

What happened exactly?

_____

Whose fault do you think it was?

_____

Reformulation

See Unit 5, Reformulation. The tape can contain a lot of reformulated work which has been done. This will include:

- the teacher's reformulations of what the student has said and written,
- the student's reformulations of what the teacher has said,
- task repetitions where the student has reformulated earlier versions of spoken tasks.

Teacher talks

Listening comprehension material of spontaneous, unscripted talks recorded on various topics by the teacher and other competent speakers can feature on the tape. (See Resources and Ideas Bank.)

Conventional coursebook use

A conventional coursebook can be used even with one student. By way of illustration, here are some possibilities using material for a pre-intermediate level student based around the topic of families. In the needs analysis the student has said that he would like to be able to make conversation about his family and relatives. He also needs practice with the past simple and past continuous for recounting anecdotes and events. Techniques discussed elsewhere in the book are used here – spoken and written reformulation, leaving the student, use of Cuisenaire rods, exploiting the empty chair, teacher–student correspondence and use of blank tapes. The activities based around the unit on the next five pages would take varying lengths of time depending on the student but should provide around six hours' work one to one.

The Family

English in Use: talking about a family

1 Look at the photograph of Sarah with her family on her wedding day. Answer the questions:

  a Who are the people in the photograph with Sarah? Try to identify her parents, grandparents, brother, sister, sister-in-law, niece, aunt and two cousins.

  b What do you think about the people in the photograph? Use some of the expressions in the box below to give your opinions.

> pleasant   interesting   in their fifties
> in his teens   worried   attractive

2 Listen to Sarah talking about her family.

  a Who do you think the people in the photograph are now?

  b Listen to the tape again and fill in the missing words.

  1 Sarah's _____ are separated.

  2 Sarah's brother is called _____ .

  3 Sarah's younger cousin works as a _____ .

  4 _____ is a heavy smoker.

  5 _____ is from New Zealand.

  6 Sarah's niece is _____ years old.

3 Talk to a partner.

　a Find out about your partner's family.

　b With the information about your partner make a family tree.

　c Ask your partner to check the family tree for mistakes.

　d Work with a group. Tell the group about your partner's family.

Skills: speaking & reading

1 Look at the photographs of Gina Trantell and her brother, Matt. They both work as models.

　a Do you think Gina looks like Matt?

　b Do you take after anyone in your family? Who and in what way?

　c Is there anyone in your family you get on really well with?

　d Is there someone you don't get on well with? Why not?

2 Before you read the text about Gina and Matt, guess the answers to these questions.

　a Do Matt and Gina like clothes?

　b How did Gina start her career as a model?

　c Is modelling different for men and women?

3 Read the article.

　a Were you right with your guesses?

　b Are the following statements true or false?

　　• Gina and Matt are very different.

　　• Their parents also work in fashion.

　　• Gina wanted to be a model all her life.

　　• Gina and Matt argued a lot when they were young.

　　• Matt sees his mother a lot.

　　• Matt and his father have a bad relationship.

　　• Matt would like to do a different job later in his life.

My family and I

BY MATT TRANTELL

My sister, Gina, takes after my mother. But I think I take after my father. He's a writer and he's always kind and cheerful.

My mother is an attractive lady who is very outgoing. She talks about her feelings a lot. She's got fair hair and deep blue eyes.

Gina has a sense of humour and gets bored very quickly. She never dresses the same way two days in a row. I find fashion very uninteresting and I never think about clothes one bit.

Gina works all over the world. We worked together once in Los

Angeles. Everywhere we went, people recognized her because her face was on the front of all the magazines.

When she was a teenager, someone saw Gina sitting in a restaurant in LA. He worked for a fashion magazine and asked Gina if she had ever thought about being a model. In fact, she had never thought about it till then. She was a normal girl like all her friends at school.

When we were young, we had fights about everything, I would rip up the posters of pop stars she had on her bedroom walls. She would throw all my clothes out of the window!

My parents are separated but they still get on well. I live in my dad's house but I see my mum at least twice a week. I get on really well with my dad. He is very relaxed and is always joking. He makes me laugh a lot. But sometimes he can be very strict.

Gina really enjoys modelling. Women earn a lot of money – far more than male models. I love modelling too, but I would rather be a professional golfer or manage a famous restaurant in London or New York. I think I have a lot of ambition. I love being successful at what I do.

4 Some of the words in the text have a short /I/ sound. For example, *sister*.

a Practise pronouncing the following words: strict, rip, bit.
b The /ɪ/ sound can have other spellings. Practise the following words: English, busy, begin, women, decided.
c Listen to the tape [Tapescript 4.2] and check your pronunciation.

Words: adjectives

Find adjectives in the text which mean:

1 happy **2** good-looking **3** boring **4** like everyone else
5 not stressed or worried

Grammar: past simple & past continuous

Past simple
Look at the picture story. This is what Anne did yesterday morning.

ring	get up	make	read	wash up	have	take

a Put the pictures in the correct order. Work with a partner.

b Now tell the story of Anne's morning using the verbs in the box:

c Put these verbs in the past simple: begin, decide, do, drink, fall, feel, go, hear, leave, play, put, sell, sing, sit, teach, walk, write.

Asking questions & giving answers

Anne **got** up at 6.   →   **Did** Anne **get** up at 6.30?
No, she **didn't**.

She **made** coffee.   →   **Did** she **make** coffee?
Yes, she **did**.

a Make questions and give answers like this about Anne. Work with another student.

Example: Anne / go out / with her cat?

Did Anne go out with her cat? No, she didn't.

1 Anne / take / a shower?
2 she / wash her clothes?
3 Anne / have / coffee for breakfast?
4 she / listen to the radio

b Ask your partner questions about yesterday morning.

Example: *Did you listen to the radio?*

Past continuous

1 Here is a sentence from the story of Anne's morning (picture f):

Anne was sleeping when the alarm clock rang.

Answer the questions about the sentence.

a Was Anne asleep before the alarm clock rang?
b Which is the short action? Which is the long action?
c Did the alarm clock interrupt Anne's sleep?

2 [Tapescript 4.3] Listen to the noises from Anne's house yesterday and answer the questions.

a What was happening?
b Which were the longer actions? Which actions interrupted them?
c Fill the gaps in the sentences about the tape.
  i When Anne _____, the birds _____ .
  ii When Anne _____ a bath, the phone _____ .
  iii She _____ the newspaper when she _____ .
d Listen to the tape [Tapescript 4.4] and check your sentences.

3 Put the verbs in brackets in the past simple or the past continuous (there is only one past continuous verb).

Anne (**1** *wake up*) _____ at 6 o'clock. She (**2** *get up*) _____ and (**3** *go*) _____ downstairs to the kitchen. She (**4** *make*) _____ some coffee. The phone (**5** *ring*) _____ while she (**6** *have*) _____ her bath. She (**7** *not answer*) _____ the phone. Later she (**8** *get dressed*) _____ and (**8** *go*) _____ for a walk with her dog.

Listen to the tape [Tapescript 4.5] and check your answers.

Grammar in use

Work with a partner. Tell your partner about:

1 your first or your last day at school
2 your first job
3 your earliest memory
4 the first time you left home
5 the first thing you bought in a shop

Exploitation of the material

English in Use: talking about a family

1 a The teacher asks the student questions about the picture in the usual way. Then she asks him to summarize everything he has said. She listens carefully and then reformulates or summarizes what he said, '*So you said...*'. Next the teacher asks him to record his summary on tape. Finally, she records her own reformulation of the student's summary.

  b The student comments on some of the people in the photograph using the words in the box. Then he repeats what he said about each of the people again as the teacher reformulates each item in writing. This means that the student dictates a sentence about each person pictured to the teacher and she writes it out, correcting errors as she does so.

2 a The exercise is followed with the student listening to see what he got right and what he got wrong. The student can be given control of the tape and left alone or the teacher can withdraw to the other side of the study room to work alone. When he is ready, the teacher asks him to give her feedback. She reformulates what he says, '*So you said...*'.

  b The student can complete the gap-fill exercise. After going over the answers, work is done on sentence stress in each answer with Cuisenaire rods. For example, the student reads the first completed sentence: '*Sarah's parents are separated.*' The teacher asks the student how many words there are and then puts down a rod to represent each word.

Sarah's   parents   are   separated.

The teacher elicits where the stresses are, i.e. on *parents* and *separated*, and places a rod on top of the second and fourth rods. Now the student practises the sentence with appropriate stress. All the gap-fill sentences 1–6 can be worked through in this way. Finally, the student records each sentence with the teacher's version directly after it.

3 a The teacher works with the student on drawing up a list of questions to ask about someone's family. The teacher asks the student the questions and reformulates/summarizes what he has said at the end. The student then asks the teacher the questions and summarizes what he has learned about the teacher's family in the same way.

b, c, d The teacher tells the student to imagine there is a friend or relative of hers sitting on an empty chair placed to one side of them. The student asks the person on the chair questions in the 'you' form about their family with a view to drawing up a family tree. The teacher replies in the 'I' form on behalf of the friend. The student then uses the family tree he has drawn up to talk about the friend's family. This is recorded on tape with a summary by the teacher recorded immediately after it. The teacher gives the student homework – he is to take the tape away and transcribe the teacher's version. Now the process is repeated with the teacher asking the student questions of a person on the imaginary chair. This time it is a friend or relative of the student. An addition to the homework is for the student to transcribe his own version for correction in the next lesson. When this correction phase has been completed, the student can read the corrected version onto tape followed by the teacher's rendition.

Skills: speaking & reading

1 The teacher pre-teaches any vocabulary from the article, *Me and my family*, which may be unknown to the student, for example, *take after, get on with, rip up, ambition, strict*.

  a, b, c, d The teacher asks the student the questions. Then the student asks the teacher the same questions.

2 The teacher introduces the article and the student guesses the answers to the questions **a–c**. The teacher writes down his guesses.

3 **a** The teacher suggests that both she and the student work alone to read the text silently to see whether his guesses are correct. The teacher can withdraw to another part of the study space. Then they discuss how close his guesses were.

  b The student reads through the true/false questions and re-reads the text to find the answers. When he is ready, the teacher asks the student to justify his answers. The teacher asks the student to put the text to one side and to summarize everything he can remember about the article. The teacher listens carefully and finally reformulates what the student said, '*So you said…*'. For homework, the student writes the teacher a letter describing the relationship between himself and a family member using the article as a guide. The student should use *take after, get on with*. When the teacher receives the letter, she replies, commenting on what he has written and writing about her relationship with a family member in the same way.

Finally, the teacher records the article while the student follows the text.

4 a The teacher models the sound in isolation and asks the student if the sound is long or short. The student repeats the sound a few times. The teacher asks the student to practise saying the three words: *strict, rip, bit.* The student says the first word once, then the teacher pronounces it and then the student repeats after the teacher's model, and so on.

b The teacher dictates the five words in question b for the student to write down. The teacher reads the words and asks the student to underline the vowels which are pronounced with the /ɪ/ sound. Then the student practises saying them. Finally the teacher records all of the words.

Words: adjectives

The teacher sets this for homework.

Grammar: past simple & past continuous

Past simple

a The student looks at the pictures and decides on the sequence. The student is then given a few minutes to think about how he will tell the story orally. He tells the story and when he has finished, the teacher reformulates his version using the past simple and recording it. The tape is played and the student stops the tape after each past simple verb, which he writes down in a column. After all the verbs have been noted, the teacher elicits the infinitive of each verb for the student to write down next to the past simple form.

b The student uses each verb in the box to make a sentence in the past simple about the story.

c The student is tested on the past simple of the verbs here and adds them to the list he made previously. Finally, the infinitive and past simple of all the verbs listed so far are recorded onto tape; the student records the infinitive followed by the teacher recording the past simple and then the list is recorded again, with the teacher reading the infinitive and the student the past simple.

Asking questions & giving answers

a The student forms the questions using the prompts 1–4 and the teacher answers. Then the teacher asks the questions and the student answers. This two-step sequence is repeated until the student can form the questions accurately. Then the student dictates the questions and answers for the teacher to write down. The questions and answers are recorded with the teacher and student taking turns to read them.

b The teacher and student work together to produce a list of ten yes/no questions in the past simple like the example in the book. The teacher fires the questions at the student, keeping a note of the answers. Then the teacher summarizes the ten things the student did or didn't do, 'So you...'. The teacher then records the summary. The process is repeated, with the student asking the questions and summarizing the events with an eventual recording. When the student records a sentence, he pauses for the teacher to reformulate it on tape.

Past continuous

1 a, b, c The teacher goes over the questions with the student.

2 a, b The teacher and student work through the tasks.

   c The student uses Cuisenaire rods to build the sentences, one word per rod. The teacher and student work on sentence stress and the weak pronunciation of *was* /wəz/. The white unit rod can be placed on top of the verbs to indicate the schwa sound /ə/. The student practises reproducing the sentences from the rods. Finally, the student and the teacher record their versions onto tape.

   d This can now be omitted, having been replaced by the work in c.

3 This can be recorded onto tape by the teacher for the student to take away as homework along with the written exercise. For example, the teacher records '*Anne*' and then in a whisper, '*wake up*', then '*one*', pauses to indicate the gap, and continues with '*at 6 o'clock*'. Alternatively, the student is given time to work on the exercise while the teacher leaves or withdraws to another part of the study area. After going over the answers, the teacher records the whole exercise, pausing for the student to say the verbs in the gaps. This can be rehearsed before the recording is made.

Grammar in use

1–5 A range of different sequences can be used here. For example:

1   your first or your last day at school

The teacher pre-records a monologue about her own experience. This should include one or two samples of the past continuous. The teacher elicits around ten questions that the student would like to ask about the teacher's first day at school. This becomes the listening task. If some of the questions are not answered on the tape, the student can ask the teacher directly. Finally, the student uses the list of questions as a prompt to summarize the information he has found out. The teacher then asks the questions about the student's experiences. The teacher summarizes/reformulates what she has heard and records this onto tape. The tape is replayed for correction and for opportunities to use the past continuous. Homework is for the student to take home the tape and reformulate his account in writing.

2   your first job

The teacher asks the student yes/no questions about his experience, e.g. *Did you have a long journey?* Finally, the teacher summarizes what she has discovered. The student talks about his experience. This is reformulated by the teacher. The student reformulates this onto tape.

3   your earliest memory

The student is given a few minutes to plan a talk. He gives the account. The teacher listens and reformulates at the end. The student repeats the task. The teacher reformulates this onto tape. The teacher gives an account of her own experiences. The student listens and reformulates at the end.

4   the first time you left home

The student gives an account. The teacher reformulates it. The student repeats the task and the teacher writes it out line by line as if taking dictation but correcting errors. Both student and teacher record the written version onto tape.

5   the first thing you bought in a shop

The student writes out the first sentence and the teacher reformulates it in writing on the line beneath. This process continues with the teacher reformulating sentence by sentence. Finally, the text is read onto tape by the teacher. The student then summarizes orally what he wrote without the script and then makes a recorded version.

cuisenaire rods

In this unit you will learn
- what Cuisenaire rods are
- how to use Cuisenaire rods
  effectively to correct your
  student
- how to use rods to clarify
  vocabulary, phonology, and
  grammar with your student
- how to use rods to get your
  student speaking

Think about

The student is given the following three Cuisenaire rods:

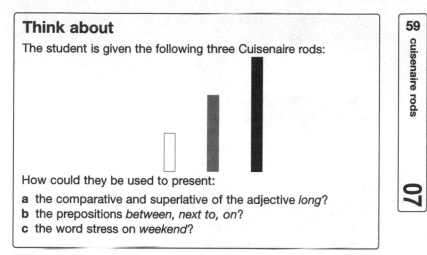

How could they be used to present:

a the comparative and superlative of the adjective *long*?
b the prepositions *between, next to, on*?
c the word stress on *weekend*?

You may have used Cuisenaire rods as a child doing maths at school. These brightly coloured, plastic or wooden rods, which measure from 1cm to 10cm in length, were invented by Georges Cuisenaire as an aid to teaching maths in primary schools and were later adopted by Caleb Gattegno, a designer of maths and reading programmes.

Gattegno was also a linguist, proficient in several languages. He advocated using the rods as part of his 'Silent Way' method of teaching language. This does not mean that the lesson should be carried out in total silence, rather that the teacher speaks only when necessary, thereby keeping her talking to a minimum – providing language models, prompting and facilitating correction.

When the student understands that the teacher is going to speak little, he is encouraged to listen carefully to what is said. Less is more. The student is not a passive recipient of information, but takes responsibility for his learning. He is challenged to think, to discover for himself, to be creative. Cuisenaire rods are objects with which the student can associate language, mediating tools which facilitate the process of learning and producing language. They can be an extension of the hands, when used to communicate. The beauty of Cuisenaire rods lies in minimalism and flexibility – they can represent almost anything: parts of words, words, people, places, objects, processes. They can simplify matters: then students may not be distracted by letters, words or spelling.

The educationalist and philosopher Rudolf Steiner believed that children benefit more from playing with simple peg dolls and blocks than with toys which come 'ready made'. Just as children 'clothe' the dolls or blocks with their imaginations, so the student's imagination is mobilized when using Cuisenaire rods.

Cuisenaire rods can be ideal for one-to-one teaching, because they provide a focus of attention which can relieve the intensity of the teacher–student relationship. They may also be effective in meeting the preferred learning channels of visual, kinaesthetic and auditory learners (see Unit 4, Learner Styles). They can be substituted, of course, with similar objects, such as Lego or other bricks.

Of course, you don't have to use 'Silent Way' to exploit Cuisenaire rods. If you have not used Cuisenaire rods before, allow yourself some time to get used to them. Experiment with different lengths and colours. Run through the sample activity sequences below in conjunction with the rods before working with a student. This will also help to anchor the sequences; practice makes perfect!

Correction techniques

Cuisenaire rods can provide a very useful and concrete way of locating and categorizing errors in order to involve the student in the process of correcting his mistakes. This may prove more useful than the teacher simply correcting the student's errors. Here are some sample correction sequences.

1 The student uses too many words

Error: *I can to fly a plane.*

The teacher 'writes' the sentence using Cuisenaire rods, eliciting each word from the student as she lays them down in a line.

Teacher   *What's the first word?*
Student   *I ...*

The teacher lays down one rod.

Teacher   *And the next?*
Student   *Can ...*

They complete the sentence. The teacher gets the student to 'read' the sentence aloud and when he gets to the rod representing 'to', the teacher indicates doubt and, if necessary, removes the rod. If the teacher cannot elicit the words by building up the sentence, she can lay down the five rods and then ask the student if he can work out what the sentence is: *I can fly a plane.*

2 The student uses too few words

Error: *He went London.*

The teacher 'writes' the sentence, eliciting each word. She then puts an extra rod in the position to be occupied by the missing word. If the student can't provide the word, the teacher can categorize the error:

Teacher   *Preposition?*

If the student still cannot provide the word, the teacher supplies it and then asks the student for the whole sentence: *He went to London.*

3 The student uses the wrong word

Error: *I became a letter this morning.*

Again, the student uses the rods to represent his sentence. The teacher asks him to 'read' it, then points to the wrong rod and categorizes the error:

Teacher   *Wrong verb. Not became. Another verb?*

The teacher provides the word, if necessary. The student may need to be told why his original choice of word is wrong. The teacher finishes by getting him to say the correct sentence: *I got a letter this morning.*

4 The student gets the word order wrong

Error: *I go every day to work.*

Again, the sentence is built up with rods and the words elicited. The teacher changes the position of the rods representing the words which are in the wrong place and gets the student to say the sentence correctly: *I go to work every day.*

5 The student puts the wrong stress on a word

■

Error: *Did you injure your leg?*

The rods representing the syllables of the word which has been wrongly stressed are laid down. The teacher categorizes the error:

Teacher   *Where's the stress?*

She asks the student to place a rod on top of the one representing the syllable which he thinks is stressed. The teacher says the word correctly and the student moves the stress rod to the correct place, i.e. on the first syllable. He says the word correctly and then says the whole sentence again.

■

Did you injure your leg?

6 The student uses the wrong sound

Error: *My hill hurts.*

The teacher uses three rods to elicit the sentence, and then points to the second rod (which should be *heel*) and indicates that the sound is wrong. She picks up a white rod and models /iː/ and places it on top of the second rod and then asks the student to try the word again. When successful, the teacher gets him to reproduce the whole sentence: *My heel hurts.*

7 The student uses inappropriate intonation

↗

Error: (asking for information) *Where do you live?*

The sentence is again represented with the rods. The teacher says the sentence with appropriate intonation and asks the student to listen:

Teacher   *Does the music go up or down?*

The teacher places one rod underneath the one representing 'live' so that the latter is tilted to show falling intonation. The student reproduces the sentence with the correct intonation.

↘

Where do you live?

Vocabulary

Colours

Perhaps the most obvious way to use the rods is to teach colours. If adopting a 'Silent Way' approach, the teacher only gives the model once (prompting correction if necessary) and provides plenty of processing time for the student. This encourages the student to think for himself and recreate the model and concentrate on the rods, which he may associate with the new vocabulary.

Sample Activity Sequence A

Aim: to clarify and focus on colour adjectives.

1 The teacher picks up a rod and says its colour once, e.g. *green*.

2 The student repeats this.

3 The teacher picks up another of the same colour and elicits the word from the student. The teacher need only repeat the word if the student cannot remember it.

4 The teacher introduces a new colour and says the word.

5 The student repeats this.

6 The teacher indicates the first colour for the student to identify.

7 The procedure continues in the same way, with words being reviewed as new ones are introduced.

8 The teacher elicits the spellings and the student writes the words down.

Options

- As practice, following the above sequence, the teacher asks, *Could you pass me a red rod?* with an appropriate gesture. The student responds by doing so and they take turns to ask for and give a rod of a specific colour. This could be combined with numbers:

    Could you pass me four green rods?

- The teacher scatters different coloured rods at random. The student says what the colours are.

- The teacher covers the rods, removes one and uncovers the rods. The student tells the teacher which one is missing.

- The teacher arranges the rods in a row that the student cannot see. She says the colours in the order in which they are arranged. The student places his rods in the same colour order. The teacher's row is revealed to compare with the student's. This can be reversed, with the student dictating the colour sequence of his rods for the teacher to reproduce.
- Starting with the colours written down, the teacher points to each one, eliciting pronunciation from the student. If this is wrong, the teacher provides the correct models. After this, the colours are introduced as in stage one of the sample activity sequence. Alternatively, the student tries to match the rods to the words.

Numbers

Sample Activity Sequence B

Aim: to clarify and focus on cardinal numbers.

1. The teacher indicates the white rod and says *one*.
2. The student repeats this.
3. The teacher introduces two white rods together and says *two*.
4. The student repeats this.
5. The teacher continues in the same way until the required numbers have been presented, she then reviews the whole set of numbers.
6. The teacher indicates the red rod and shows that two white rods are the same length as one red one. She indicates the white rod and elicits *one*. She points to the two white rods and elicits *two*. She replaces the two white rods with a red one and elicits *two* – so now the red rod represents number two.
7. The teacher introduces three white rods together and says *three*.
8. The student repeats this.
9. The teacher reviews *one*, *two* and *three* before replacing the three white rods with a green one.
10. This pattern continues, with numbers constantly being reviewed.

Options

- Once this has got underway, the student takes responsibility for replacing the white rods with coloured rods, with the teacher only needing to provide the language.

- Ordinal numbers (1st, 2nd, 3rd) can be introduced in a similar way. The teacher uses three rods to represent participants in a race, briefly 'racing' them, so that it is clear that one has come first, one second, and one third. She then places the athletes on a podium built of other rods. The rods representing the participants are placed on the podium one at a time and the relevant ordinal given.

Representing words

Cuisenaire rods can also be used to represent words, e.g. nouns, verbs, prepositions.

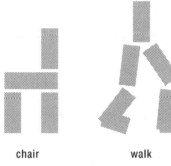

chair

walk

through

At higher levels, students can use the rods to symbolize their interpretations of abstract nouns, e.g. beauty, confusion. For the teacher, this might give a useful indication of how much the student has understood, while the student is provided with a valuable insight into the nuances of meaning. It is, therefore, a useful revision technique.

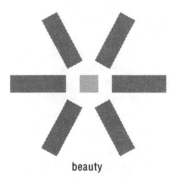

beauty

Teacher   *Here is a list of the words which were in the text you read yesterday. I'm going to choose one of these words, but I'm not going to tell you which one it is. I'm going to use these rods to represent my understanding of the word. Which word am I representing?*

Sample Activity Sequence C

Aim: to revise meaning and pronunciation of vocabulary.

1 The teacher provides a list of words to be revised and explains that she is going to use the rods to show an interpretation of one of the words.

2 The student watches while she does this. The student tells the teacher which word he thinks is being shown. The teacher prompts him to correct his pronunciation if necessary.

3 The student arranges the rods to show his interpretation of the same word. Teacher and student discuss their different interpretations.

4 The student chooses another word and uses the rods to represent his interpretation of its meaning. The teacher guesses which word it is.

5 The pattern is repeated for as long as the student finds it interesting.

Options

- The teacher uses the rods to review a vocabulary set recently taught, e.g. *bungalow, detached house, block of flats*. Either teacher or student represents these with the rods.

- Collocations can be practised in a similar way. For example, the language used to describe trends (a rapid decline, a steady increase) and language taken from a newspaper article – to clear one's name, to break one's silence, the run up to the election.

a rapid decline

- The various meanings of phrasal verbs can be shown with rods.

- A cline (a sliding scale of degree) can be demonstrated, e.g. adjectives: *peckish, hungry, famished*; as can adverbs of frequency: *never, occasionally, sometimes, usually, always*.

- The student arranges the rods to show his interpretation of a text. This might be abstract or more concrete. For example, the student reads a description of an orchestra and arranges the rods to show his comprehension. Alternatively, the rods are used to represent a manufacturing process or the distribution of goods described in business documents or a company brochure, a recipe from a cookery book, instructions from a manual, or directions to someone's house taken from a letter.

Settings and situations

Not all nouns are best represented with Cuisenaire rods. Pointing to a black rod and calling it 'mother' is not much help to the complete beginner. Rods are not always a suitable replacement for realia or pictures. However, vocabulary which relates to objects in fixed situations can be taught using Cuisenaire rods.

Sample Activity Sequence D

Aim: to clarify and focus on vocabulary in a restaurant.

1 The teacher sets the scene, for example, *We're in a restaurant*, and sits at the table with the student. She arranges the rods on the table in the form of two place settings. Some rods represent cutlery, some plates and so on.

2 The teacher picks up one of the rods, performs a cutting motion with it and elicits or presents what it is: *knife.*

3 The student repeats this.

4 The teacher introduces the language one item at a time, reviewing along the way by pointing to rods and eliciting the words they represent.

5 The teacher introduces the situational aspect and elicits the process: *What happens when you arrive in a restaurant? What happens first? And then?* (you come into a restaurant, the waiter asks if you have made a reservation or how many people there are, shows you to your table, gives you a menu...)

6 The student summarizes the language and the teacher reformulates it. (See Unit 5, Reformulation.)

Options
• Other suitable fixed locations and situations include:
   a **church wedding** (altar, bride, best man, to walk down the aisle);
   a **driving lesson** or manoeuvre in a car (steering wheel, gear stick, to reverse, to indicate);

a **procedure on a computer** (keyboard, mouse, to log on, to click on);
going into a shop (till, counter, fitting room, to sign);
in a supermarket (trolley, check out, to park in the car park);
changing money or opening an account **at a bank** (currency, statement, to withdraw money);
buying tickets **at a railway station** (ticket office, single);
going to the **theatre or cinema** (circle, intermission, row, to reserve).

- The lesson could go on to include dialogue building relevant to the situation, e.g. a conversation between a waitress and a customer ordering food, after the restaurant vocabulary and processes have been introduced. (See Sample Activity Sequence D).

Speaking

Choosing to study English one to one may not mean that the student likes being or wants to be the focus of attention all the time. At the beginning of the course, particularly, he may find the experience of being the only student somewhat nerve-wracking. He is likely to feel more comfortable talking about familiar subjects (family, friends, job, workplace and so on). In these areas, it is the student and not the teacher who is the expert. At lower levels, the student can point to the rod and communicate with little vocabulary, maybe just one word (no need for grammar). For example, when describing and representing a room using rods, the student points to rods and says *my bed, CD player*. The Cuisenaire rods provide a welcome diversion, tools on which both student and teacher can focus their attention. Furthermore, instead of sitting and thinking things through, worrying that he might appear to be doing nothing, the student can formulate ideas while arranging the rods.

Promoting fluency: family

The teacher starts things off by describing her family, the members of which are represented by rods.

Sample Activity Sequence E

Aim: to clarify, focus on and provide restricted use of vocabulary of family and to provide practice in spoken fluency talking about family.

1 The teacher introduces her family, using (different coloured) rods to represent the different members. She includes as much detail as is appropriate for the level of the student.

Teacher   *This is me* (green rod). *I have a sister* (red rod) *and two brothers* (yellow rods). *These are my parents* (pink rods).

Depending on the level of the student, the teacher can add more information – *My sister works in a department store in Paris. She's lived in France for two years now* (and so on).

2 The student summarizes what the teacher has said.

3 The student describes his family in the same way.

4 The teacher reformulates what the student has said orally and/or in writing.

Options

- The rods are arranged in the form of a family tree.
- The rods can be placed nearer or further from the rod representing the teacher/student to show how emotionally close the family members are.
- The teacher introduces members of the extended family: in-laws, half sisters, step brothers and so on. By starting off with the nuclear family, the teacher will be able to build on these relationships. If the student is familiar with *mother* and *sister*, *aunt* will be easy to introduce.
- Friends or colleagues can be substituted for family members.
- The student could go on to produce a written version of what he has said.
- Stage 3 could be recorded on to tape and then re-recorded following the teacher's reformulation.

Promoting fluency: places

Sample Activity Sequence F

Aim: to clarify and focus on vocabulary relating to streets and to provide practice in talking about where people live.

1 The teacher describes the area surrounding her home (the street, bus stop, shops and so on), bringing rods into play as she goes along.

This is my house. Here's the garden with two apple trees. This is my street – it's a cul de sac. And there's a shop on the corner which is open every day until 10 and sells everything ...

2 The student summarizes this information, referring to the arrangements of rods.

3 The student then describes the area surrounding his home.

4 The teacher reformulates this in the same way.

Options

- Describing any room in a house, including furnishings.
- Describing the inside of the house.
- Describing the student's street, town, region, country.
- Describing work premises.
- Describing processes, e.g. manufacturing processes, a production line.
- Combining a description of a process with a description of the work premises is also a possibility. For example, a student who is a nurse or doctor could describe the layout of the casualty department and the admission procedure for a patient.
- Describing the hierarchy of the student's work place.
- Giving and following directions when a series of streets or part of a town have been built up with rods.

Promoting fluency: creating a scene

Sample Activity Sequence G

Aim: to practise oral fluency.

1 The teacher constructs an environment without telling the student what it is (perhaps part of a busy city, with an arch, a broad street, some towers and so on).

2 The teacher asks the student to describe the scene and gives prompts to encourage detail:

So what is this? What colour is it? Tell me more ...

Of course, the student's interpretation might be different from what the teacher had in mind. The final version is recorded on to tape.

3 The teacher plays the recording and stops the tape when errors are made. (She might want to decide on criteria first to avoid correcting everything. Criteria could be sounds, stress, verb forms and so on.) The teacher elicits or gives correct language.

4 The student records a second version of this interpretation.

5 The student creates a scene of his own, which the teacher interprets.
6 The student reformulates what the teacher has said.
7 The student describes what he was actually constructing.

Options
- The student interprets the teacher's arrangement of rods once without being recorded, giving him the opportunity to 'rehearse'. The lesson then continues as in 2 above.
- The student listens to the recording and reformulates it in writing.
- The student later writes his description of either scene.
- The student provides an oral comparison of the two interpretations of the same scene.
- The student writes a comparison of the two descriptions of the same scene.

Promoting fluency: story telling

Cuisenaire rods are very useful tools for story telling. The teacher can use this as a device for encouraging fluency by enacting a whole narrative with the rods. The student watches and then retells the story without interruption. Alternatively, the teacher can elicit a sentence at a time and work on accuracy. The teacher can establish what each rod represents before beginning the story or introduce them as she goes along.

Sample Activity Sequence H

Aim: to practise oral fluency by telling a story.

1 The teacher places a number of green rods upright on the table to represent a thick wood and says:
    This is a wood. or *What do you think this is?*
2 The teacher introduces two red rods, establishes that these represent children and asks:
    Is this a boy or a girl? about each.
3 The two characters are moved about, with one being placed behind a tree, to indicate that they are playing hide and seek.
4 The children move deeper into the wood, playing their game. Eventually, the seeker cannot find the one who is hiding. She runs off to fetch help in the shape of a pink rod, representing a parent.

5 The parent makes the child stay outside the wood and searches for the hidden child.
6 There is jubilation when the lost child is found, depicted by the three rods dancing!
7 The teacher hands the rods over to the student who uses them to retell the story orally.

Options

- The student retells the story without using the rods.
- There can, of course, be more detail in the story, involving other characters, such as police officers. The student could go on to write a newspaper report of what happened.
- The story can be retold from the point of view of different characters.
- The teacher encourages the student to include more detail, such as descriptions of the people, the scenery, the weather and so on.
- The teacher introduces new language by reformulating the student's version of the story with adjectives, adverbs, discourse markers, narrative tenses and so on.
- The teacher works on phonological aspects of the narrative, such as sentence stress, intonation.
- The story need not be fictional; there simply needs to be a sequence of events. It could be something as simple as the student's morning routine or what he did one day on his last holiday (*I swam in the sea, I sunbathed, I went sightseeing* …). A particular tense could be practised (present simple for habits/routines and so on).
- The teacher elicits the story line by line: *What happened next?* The student repeats the first sentence, then adds the second, repeats the first and second sentences, adds the third and so on.
- The student prepares a story (perhaps for homework) and tells it with the aid of the rods.
- After reading a narrative, the student/teacher retells the storyline using the rods.
- The teacher cuts up a story into sentences for the student to sequence. The student then uses the rods to retell the story. Alternatively, the teacher gives the student the jumbled sentences, enacts the story silently with the rods and this helps the student to sequence the narrative.

Dialogue building

Sample Activity Sequence I

Aim: to practise clothes shop language.

1 The teacher sets the scene (e.g. in a clothes shop) and assigns roles. The teacher begins the dialogue playing her part and then elicits the student's lines.

> **Teacher** *This is a clothes shop. You are the customer. I am the shop assistant. 'Good morning. Can I help you?' What do you say?*
>
> **Student** *Good morning. I'm looking for a T-shirt.*

The teacher uses an appropriate correction technique as necessary, asks the student how many words there are in the new sentence and builds it up using the rods. The teacher points to each rod and re-elicits the whole sentence word by word.

2 The teacher re-runs the dialogue from the beginning.

> **Teacher** *So ... Good morning. Can I help you?*
>
> **Student** *I'm looking for a T-shirt.*

3 The dialogue continues.

> **Teacher** *What size are you, sir?*
>
> **Student** *Medium.*

The teacher uses the rods as before to standardize and re-elicits the new line.

4 The dialogue is then reviewed from the beginning. The teacher refers to the lines of rods as necessary to prompt or correct the student.

> **Teacher** *Good morning. Can I help you?*
>
> **Student** *I'm looking for a T-shirt.*
>
> **Teacher** *What size are you, sir?*
>
> **Student** *Medium.*

5 The dialogue is built up line by line in this way until it reaches an appropriate length.

6 Finally, the dialogue can be recorded on tape and/or written up.

Options

- Additional rods are used to show sentence stress or intonation. (See Phonology.)
- Single rods can be used to represent entire phrases, once the student is familiar with each one.

Phonology

Sounds: minimal pairs

Students who are having difficulty distinguishing between English phonemes which do not exist in their native languages may need plenty of exposure to those sounds before they can be expected to produce them. An Italian, for example, may be unable to tell the difference between the minimal pair /ɪ/ and /iː/, as in *fit* and *feet*, because the nearest sound in Italian is somewhere between the two. At a very basic level, different coloured Cuisenaire rods can represent the two sounds, with the student simply pointing to the rod which represents the sound he hears. When contrasting a long and short sound, a long and short rod can be used. There is no need for the student to try to make these sounds himself at this stage but he can be involved in production later.

Sample Activity Sequence J

Aim: to clarify, focus on and practise the sounds /ɪ/ and /iː/.

1 The teacher picks up a rod and makes the sound /ɪ/.
2 The teacher picks up a longer rod and makes the sound /iː/.
3 The teacher repeats the sounds randomly and each time the student has to point to the rod which represents the sound he hears. This continues until the student is able to identify the sounds with confidence.
4 A third, differently coloured rod is introduced. Now the student produces the sounds for the teacher to identify by indicating the appropriate rod representing the sound she hears. If the sound the student makes does not correspond to either phoneme, the teacher points to the new third rod.
5 The teacher introduces two lists of one syllable words which contain one or other of the sounds: e.g. *sit, lip, lid, seat, leap, lead*. The teacher reads these to the student: first the words containing the short sound, then those containing the long and finally alternating between the two lists.
6 The teacher then says one of these words at random and the student points to the rod which represents the phoneme he hears. They do this several times until the student can accurately identify the words.
7 The student has now had exposure to the sounds within words. The teacher points to words on the lists and the student says the words. If the student does not produce the correct sound, the teacher can point to the appropriate rod as a correction technique.

8 Now the student says the words at random and the teacher points to the appropriate rod. If the word produced by the student does not contain either phoneme, the teacher points to the third rod as in stage four.

Options

- Sentences including words which contain the relevant phonemes are introduced. Until now, the student has been able to concentrate on individual words, but he needs practice in producing these words among others.
- The teacher encourages the student to notice how her face moves when making the two sounds, e.g. the position of the tongue, the teeth, how the lips and jaw move.
- The student looks at the teacher's mouth and then at his own in a mirror while he is forming the sound.
- If appropriate for the sounds the teacher mouths the phonemes silently and the student identifies the sounds by pointing to the correct rod, so that he is forced to focus on the manner of articulation.
- The teacher makes the sounds facing away from the student or with her mouth hidden for the student to identify, so that he is forced to concentrate on the sound.

Sounds: consonant clusters

Some learners have difficulty producing two or more consonants together. Thais, for example, may find *cr*, *fl* at the beginnings of words very hard to say and often miss out the second consonant. Consonant clusters at the ends of words – *nd*, for example – may also be problematic. It is not always the individual sounds which create difficulties but the combination of sounds. Different rods can be used for two such consonant sounds. Once the individual sounds have been established, the rods can be moved closer together to reflect what happens with the sounds.

Sample Activity Sequence K

Aim: to clarify, focus on and practise the consonant cluster /kr/.

1 The teacher indicates a rod and says /k/.
2 The student repeats this.
3 The teacher points to a differently coloured rod and says /r/.
4 Again, the student repeats the sound.

5 The teacher points to each rod in turn, with the student making the relevant sounds.
6 The teacher points from one rod to the other faster and faster, also moving them closer and closer together, so that the student is compelled to produce the sounds closer together.
7 If the student is tripping over his tongue, the teacher could start again and pick up speed more gradually. The two sounds should blend and not seem to have another sound intruding between them.
8 The student is presented with a list of words containing the relevant consonant cluster and practises saying these. He may find it helpful to move the two rods towards each other as before.

Options
- The same process can be used for practising diphthongs, e.g. /əʊ/ in boat and /aɪ/ in fine, providing the student is able to produce the two single sounds (/ə/, /u/ and /æ/, /ɪ/) first.

Sounds: voiced and unvoiced

Many learners of English are unable to distinguish between voiced and unvoiced sounds, for example /g/ and /k/. The movements of the tongue and jaw look the same, but the voice box is used in the production of the former and not the latter. By placing your fingers over your voice box, you can feel it vibrating when you utter a voiced sound. Again, using Cuisenaire rods provides a visual anchor.

Sample Activity Sequence L

Aim: to clarify, focus on and practise /g/ and /k/.

1 The teacher uses two rods of the same colour, because the production of the two sounds uses the same parts of the mouth. She places them upright on the table.
2 The teacher points to one of the rods and makes the unvoiced sound /k/, then points to the other rod and places a white rod on top of it, making the voiced sound /g/.
3 The teacher repeats this.
4 The teacher produces the sounds randomly for the student to recognize. He points to the appropriate rod when the teacher makes the sounds. They do this several times.
5 The teacher draws the student's attention to the difference in producing the two sounds. The teacher gets the student to place his fingers on his voice box and make a number of 'uh'

and 'ah' sounds, so that he feels the voice box vibrating. Once he realizes that some sounds are produced with the aid of the voice box and some are not, he is ready for the next stage.

6 With the fingers of one hand on her throat, the teacher points to the single rod, makes the sound /k/ and tells the student that her voice box is not vibrating or shows this by shaking her head. She then points to the rod which has the white one on top, makes the sound /g/ and either tells the student or nods her head to show that the voice box is vibrating.

7 The student tries this, so that he can feel the difference and matches the sounds to the rods.

8 The teacher provides a list of words which contain the two sounds and says the words and again the student identifies the sounds by pointing to the rods.

9 Now it is the student's turn to read the words for the teacher to identify with the rods in the same way.

Options
• The student is introduced to a number of the minimal pairs containing voiced and unvoiced phonemes. He sorts them into two groups: voiced or unvoiced.

Word stress

Where a word has two syllables or more, one of those will carry the primary stress. This means that the syllable is longer and louder than the others and that there is a change in pitch. For example, *water* is stressed on the first syllable. Words which are incorrectly stressed may be incomprehensible. Cuisenaire rods provide a helpful visual for those who 'can't hear' stress.

Sample Activity Sequence M

Aim: to clarify, focus on and practise word stress.

1 The teacher selects the words she wants to practise.

2 The teacher lays out four rods to represent the syllables of one of the words, e.g. *photographer*. She says the word and points to each syllable as she is saying it.

3 The teacher repeats this, placing an identical rod on top of the rod representing the stressed syllable.

4 The teacher indicates that the student should repeat this.

5 If the student stresses the wrong syllable, the teacher points to the rod representing the syllable which carries the stress.

6 The student tries again and the process is repeated for the remaining words.

Options

- The student listens to the teacher saying the word(s) and demonstrates where he thinks the stress is as above.
- The teacher writes the word and asks the student to 'show' it in terms of the number of syllables, marking stress as above.
- The student is confused about the number of syllables in a word and misrepresents it. For example, he puts down four rods for *comfortable* (/kʌmfɔ:teɪbəl/), rather than three (/kʌmftəbəl/). In this case, the teacher removes one of the rods. The student tries to say the word correctly.
- The rods can be placed upright, so that stressed syllables are taller.
- The rods can be placed upright, with a white rod again put on top of the stressed syllable.
- The rods can be laid flat, with only the one representing the stressed syllable standing upright.
- The student matches words to rod patterns.

Sounds: the *schwa*

This is the most common sound in the English language. It appears frequently in the unstressed syllables of words. For example, it is the final sound in the word *dinner* (where *din* is stressed). It also appears in weak forms of words which have both a strong and a weak pronunciation: prepositions (*from, to, for*); modal verbs (*can, must, could*); articles (*the, a*) and conjunctions (*and, but*), auxiliaries (*does, have*).

For example, the preposition *of* in final position – e.g. *What does it consist of?* – has a strong pronunciation /ɒv/. However, it has a weak pronunciation when it is part of a phrase such as *a cup of tea* (/əkʌpəvti:/). This is something the student needs to be aware of to understand native speakers. There is a school of thought which says that a student does not need to be able to produce weak forms to be intelligible. The student may be stressing the wrong syllable of a word or placing equal stress on all syllables. By replacing a syllable containing a *schwa* with the smallest rod, the teacher is showing that the sound is short and weak.

Sample Activity Sequence N

Aim: to clarify, focus on and practise the *schwa* sound.

1 The teacher selects the words she wants to practise.
2 The teacher says a word, such as *photograph*, and lays out the rods according to the number of syllables the word has (so that the student understands that there are three in this case). The teacher says the word and quickly replaces the middle rod with a white one to represent the *schwa*, then repeats the word, pointing to the rods as she says each syllable.
3 The student says the word. If he says it with the wrong stress or without the *schwa*, the teacher draws his attention to the white rod and repeats the word herself. The student tries again.
4 The teacher says a number of words and each time the student represents its syllables using rods, including the white one to represent the *schwa*, saying the words as well.

Options

- The student is not expected to say the words, only to arrange the rods with the white one in the right place. Some students find it very difficult to produce the *schwa* sound and some would argue that it is not necessary for them to do so. However, knowing of its existence will help with understanding native speakers. This option would be a good one to start with, as it provides the student with exposure to the sound without expecting him to produce it. (The same applies to all sounds, of course, not only the *schwa*.)
- The teacher says nothing. The student refers to a written list of the words and arranges the rods according to how he thinks the word is stressed and also indicating the *schwa* with a white rod.
- Whole sentences can be tackled in the same way. The white rod can be used to highlight the *schwa* in some auxiliary verbs, such as the weak form of *does* /dəz/ and *can* /kən/; the weak form of conjunctions, e.g. *and* /ənd/ and *but* /bət/; the weak form of prepositions, e.g. *for* /fə/ and *to* /tə/.

Sentence stress

Generally speaking, proficient speakers naturally stress the words which carry the meaning of the sentence (nouns and verbs, rather than articles, pronouns, auxiliary verbs and prepositions, which are necessary for grammar). As a rule of thumb, the words which are unstressed could be omitted, leaving the stressed words to convey the message, somewhat like a telegram. For example,

I was riding my bike when I slipped on some ice.

Depending on context, the words which we would naturally stress are *riding, bike, slipped* and *ice.* The normal stress in words of more than one syllable does not change. *Riding* is stressed on the first syllable. In sentence stress, it is still a question of stressing the right syllable in each word. Try saying the sentence while beating time. The syllables in between the stressed ones are unstressed.

Sample Activity Sequence O

Aim: to clarify, focus on and practise sentence stress.

1 The teacher selects the sentences to be worked on. An idea here is to build in an element of context by setting the scene, e.g. *There are two friends in a room and one offers the other a cup of tea.*

    A *Would you like a cup of tea?*
    B *No, coffee, please.*

2 The teacher lays out a number of rods, each of which represents a word in the target sentences. The teacher reads the sentences aloud and asks the student to identify the stressed words, i.e. *like, cup, tea, no, coffee* and *please.* The teacher places a rod on top of each of the rods representing the stressed words.

3 The teacher invites the student to practise the sentences. They take turns at reading parts **A** and **B** of the dialogue.

Options

- The student shows the stresses where he thinks they would be, without hearing the teacher say the sentence first.
- The teacher can combine reading the sentence with beating time. This way, the student will see that unstressed words are often said quickly in order to fit in with the beat.
- A similar process can be used to show how stress shifts according to meaning. Even a simple sentence such as *My mother is a doctor* can be stressed in several different ways, perhaps in response to a question. If the teacher asks, *What*

does your mother do? the stress will be on *doctor*. In response to *Your mother isn't a doctor!* the student will move the stress marker to *is*.

- Instead of, or as well as, focusing on stressed syllables, the teacher can use rods to denote the weak ones (see the *schwa*, above).
- Sentence stress can be incorporated into dialogue building. (See Sample Activity Sequence I).

Intonation

Cuisenaire rods can be used as a visual representation of intonation – where the tone of voice rises and falls. One rod is used as a rest on which to place one end of another, so that the latter is tilted. Depending on whether it tilts up or down on the right, the intonation of the word will be shown to rise or fall. Asking 'yes/no' questions, one has a rising tone at the end of the sentence:

Have you ever been to Spain?

Sample Activity Sequence P

Aim: to clarify, focus on and practise the rising tunes of 'yes/no' questions

1 The teacher dictates the beginnings of a number of 'yes/no' questions:
   Are you ...?, Have you ...?, Do you ...? and so on.
2 The student completes the questions in writing to ask the teacher, who could check on accuracy before the next stage.
3 The teacher asks the student to represent his first question using rods – one for each word.
4 The student asks the teacher his first question.
5 The teacher places a white rod underneath the end of the last word, so that the rod is tilting up on the right. The teacher asks the question, pointing to the tilting rod to draw attention to the rising intonation at the end of the question.
6 The student repeats the question.
7 The student asks the remaining questions, with the teacher only answering if the student remembers the rising tone at the end. The teacher can point to the tilted rod to remind the student to do this if he forgets.

Options

- The falling tone at the end of a *wh* question, asking for new information, can be shown in a similar way, for example *Where do you live?* Similarly, rising tunes can be shown on *wh* questions asking for repetition or clarification and polite request forms. The rising and falling tunes on tag questions can also be demonstrated.
- A mixture of 'yes/no' and *wh* questions are dealt with in the same lesson.
- Intonation can be incorporated into dialogue building. (See Sample Activity Sequence I.)

Connected speech

Cuisenaire rods help learners to see how many proficient speakers connect words in normal speech. These connections are often the reason learners have problems understanding spoken English. One example of connected speech is when the last sound of one word is a consonant and the first sound of the next is a vowel, e.g. *He's⌣an⌣engineer.* This is known as catenation. While it is not essential for learners of English to speak in this way, it is important for them to know that many people do, which is why it can be difficult to know where one word ends and another begins.

Sample Activity Sequence Q

Aim: to clarify, focus on and practise catenation.

1 The teacher either focuses on a phrase or sentence of the student's or presents one of her own, e.g. *I'm interested in art and history.* The teacher uses rods to represent the sentence, eliciting each word from the student. The rods are not touching each other at this stage. The student 'reads' the whole sentence.

2 The teacher pushes the first two rods together, saying the words: *I'm⌣interested*, which the student repeats. The teacher pushes the first two rods together with the third, eliciting *I'm⌣interested in* and continues like this until the rods representing the first five words are touching.

3 The teacher asks the student whether or not the last rod should be touching the one before it, and then either elicits or gives the explanation that the first four words are touching because of the consonant to vowel link, but that the final sound of *and* and the first sound of *history* are both consonants.

4 The student tries to 'read' the whole sentence with catenation.

Options

- Pairs of words where the last sound of one is the same as the first sound of the next, e.g. *bus stop* can be dealt with in a similar way. White rods representing the /s/ are placed at the end of one rod and the beginning of the next. One is removed and the three rods pushed together to show that there is no break between the words.

bu-s   s-top   bu-s-top

- Whenever you are working with sentences, such as in dialogue building, features of connected speech can be highlighted in this way.

Grammar

Cuisenaire rods are also extremely helpful visual and kinaesthetic tools when teaching grammar and structure.

Prepositions of place

Sample Activity Sequence R

Aim: to clarify, focus on and practise prepositions of place.

1 The teacher builds a simple bridge using three rods, and makes a box shape, with sides at least two rods deep.
2 The teacher drops a white rod into the box and says:
   Where is the rod? or
   What's the preposition?
   If the student does not know, the teacher says *in* and the student repeats this.
3 The teacher puts the white rod on the bridge and elicits or gives *on*, which the student repeats.
4 The teacher puts the white rod back into the box to re-elicit *in*.
5 This continues, in the same way, illustrating other prepositions, such as *next to*, *near*, *on top of*, *between*, *opposite* and *behind*.

Options

- The teacher builds the prepositions into sentences, such as, *The rod is in the box*, which the student repeats. (The student must be pre-taught the word 'box'.)

- The teacher asks questions, such as *Where is the rod?* in order to elicit a response.
- The teacher asks questions, such as *Is the rod under the bridge?* in order to elicit both positive and negative sentences. (The student must be pre-taught the word 'bridge'.)
- The student places the rods in the positions designated by the teacher. (A timid student may benefit from not having to speak.)
- The teacher builds a simple construction using no more than five rods, which the student cannot see. The teacher then gives instructions for the student to build an identical structure. (At higher levels, using slightly more complex language, this works better if the teacher does not watch what the student is doing.) The roles are then reversed.
- The student can follow instructions from a written text or tape, for example *Put three green rods down in a row. Place a red rod on top of the green rod in the centre.*
- The target language may be imperatives – for example *Put the red rod next to the blue rod* – in which case a similar format can be used. Request language can also be used – for example *Could you put the red rod next to the blue rod, please?*
- The teacher gives instructions, such as *Put one red rod on top of another*, following instructions herself and inviting the student to do so at the same time.

Articles

The articles, *the* (definite article), *a* and *an* (indefinite article) and zero article, may prove difficult for learners whose languages do not have them (e.g. Polish, Turkish, Japanese). On the other hand, they can still be problematic for learners whose languages do have them (e.g. French, German, Italian), as they are used in different ways.

Sample Activity Sequence S

Aim: to clarify, focus on and practise articles.

1 The teacher begins by saying, *We're practising 'a', 'an' and 'the'*. The teacher puts a number of the rods of one colour on the table. Pointing to them, she says: *You want this one. What do you say?*

2 The student replies, without pointing, *Can I have a rod?* If he does not know how to use the article, the teacher gives him the sentence.
3 The teacher places a number of rods, (e.g. four red and one white) on the table. Pointing to the white one, she says: *You want this one. What do you say?*
4 The student, again without pointing, replies: *Can I have the white rod?* The teacher gives him this sentence if he does not know.
5 The stages are repeated.

Options

- As a discrimination task, the teacher reads a sentence with articles and zero articles and the student represents the sentence as he hears it. He then reads back the sentence to show whether or not he has heard all the articles.

Structures: comparatives and superlatives

Sample Activity Sequence T

Aim: to clarify, focus on and practise comparative adjectives.

1 The teacher places a rod (e.g. orange) upright on the table; then places another (e.g. black) next to it and says: *Are they the same or different?* and elicits the difference.
2 The teacher goes on to elicit: *The black rod is shorter than the orange rod*.
3 The teacher continues with other pairs of rods to elicit the comparatives again.

Options

- The same format can be used to clarify and focus on superlatives, e.g. *The orange rod is the tallest.*
- An alternative is to involve the student in comparing, for example, towns, countries, people and buildings. The rods can then be used to show the structure of the sentence. A short rod is used to represent the suffix *-er* or rods can be used to represent *the* and *-est*.

Structures: telling the time

Cuisenaire rods can take the place of a clock face.

Sample Activity Sequence U

Aim: to clarify, focus on and practise asking and giving clock time.

1 The teacher lays down four white rods to represent the quarters of a clock face. Other rods are used to represent the hands.
2 The teacher begins by showing, for example, 5 o'clock and asking: *What's the time?* to elicit the target language.
   A number of 'o'clocks' are practised like this. Then the student takes a turn to ask the question and the teacher replies.
3 The teacher introduces the half hour, which is practised several times. The 'o'clocks' are reviewed.
4 The teacher introduces the quarters past and to the hour, constantly reviewing what has come before. Again, the roles are reversed.

Options

- The teacher uses the clock face in conjunction with her routine. *I get up at 7.30. I have lunch at 1.00.* Either she moves the hands and elicits the time, or she says the time, and the student moves the hands.
- The student describes his day, moving the hands of the clock.

Auxiliaries

Cuisenaire rods can be used to demonstrate the various uses of auxiliary verbs. These include:

negatives: *He **doesn't** like country music.*
questions: ***Have** you finished?*
question tags: *It's hot in here, **isn't** it?*
short answers: *Yes, I **do**.*
verb forms: *She **is** reading.*

The teacher may choose to use the rods to present or review structures. The following lesson demonstrates the presentation of forming questions in the third person of the present simple:
   Does he wear a uniform?

Sample Activity Sequence V

Aim: to clarify, focus on and practise 'yes/no' questions in the third person singular of the present simple.

1 The teacher shows a picture of a police officer and elicits a statement in the present simple, e.g. *He wears a uniform*.

2 She indicates that the student should arrange the rods to represent this statement, using a different colour for each word. The third person -*s* should be clear, perhaps represented by a white rod.

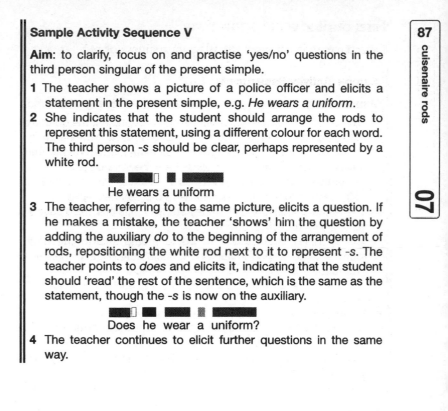

He wears a uniform

3 The teacher, referring to the same picture, elicits a question. If he makes a mistake, the teacher 'shows' him the question by adding the auxiliary *do* to the beginning of the arrangement of rods, repositioning the white rod next to it to represent -*s*. The teacher points to *does* and elicits it, indicating that the student should 'read' the rest of the sentence, which is the same as the statement, though the -*s* is now on the auxiliary.

Does he wear a uniform?

4 The teacher continues to elicit further questions in the same way.

Options

- The question forms for the other subjects (*I*, *you*, *we*, *they*) can be dealt with in a similar way, without the white rod representing -*s*, of course.

- The past simple of regular verbs can be tackled in a similar way, e.g. *She watched television. Did she watch television?*

- The rods representing the subject and verb need to change places when presenting the present simple question form of *to be*, e.g. *He is happy. Is he happy?*

- A similar procedure can be followed for negative forms, e.g. *He smokes. He doesn't smoke.*

Verb endings

This activity sequence presents the past simple of regular verbs.

Sample Activity Sequence W

Aim: to clarify, focus on and practise the past simple of regular verbs.

1 The teacher shows the student pictures of a person doing about five different activities and elicits what the person did the previous day. The teacher records what he says on tape.

   Teacher *Tell me about Neale's day yesterday.*

   Student *He wash his car. He paint a picture. He play his piano.*

2 The student listens to the tape, stopping it when he hears a verb, which he writes down.

3 The teacher gestures that the student should lay down a rod to represent one of the regular verbs, such as *walk*.

4 The teacher hands him another rod, indicates that he should add it to the end of the *walk* rod and says, *walked*. The student repeats this.

5 The teacher uses a different colour rod to represent each verb, but the same colour to represent the *-ed* ending. This emphasizes the regularity of the spelling of the verb ending.

6 The student reformulates his original recording orally or in writing or both.

Options

- The *-ed* ending is represented by two white rods (one for each letter). The letters may be written on in pencil with wooden rods or with a felt tip on plastic rods.

- The teacher draws the student's attention to the three different sounds of the *-ed* ending /t/, /d/ and /ɪd/. These are represented with three different rods. The teacher 'dictates' the verbs to the student, who adds the rod representing the appropriate verb ending.

- At stage 1, the teacher asks the student what he did the previous day and uses the student's own verbs. While this is more meaningful for the student, the risk is that some, most or even all of the verbs will be irregular.

- The past forms of irregular verbs are shown as a completely different colour from the present (such as *goes*, *went*) and do not have a different coloured rod for the ending.

- Other verb endings can be presented or reviewed in a similar way: third person *-s*, *-ing*.

08

cards and reusable laminated cards

In this unit you will learn

- how to use cards to aid your student's speaking, pronunciation, vocabulary, grammar and reading
- how to play language games with your student

Think about

The student is given six cards with one of the following items written on each:

always	*never*	*hardly ever*
often	*occasionally*	*sometimes*

How could these be used for language purposes?

Like Cuisenaire rods, cards and laminated cards provide visual and kinaesthetic learners with tools which can greatly aid the learning process. They can be made easily and are cheaper than Cuisenaire rods – though they will not last as long and are not necessarily an alternative.

The cards can be the small, ivory cards bought in stationery shops, blank postcards or homemade. In each case, they are written or drawn on and used as stimuli for speaking or to help with accuracy. They can, of course, be used over and over again with different students. Covering them with clear, adhesive plastic will keep them clean. In this book, they are referred to simply as cards.

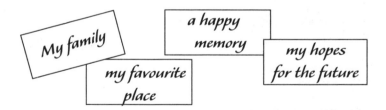

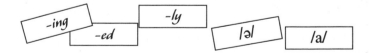

The reusable laminated cards are simply strips of paper or card which have either been laminated or covered in adhesive, clear plastic. They can be written on with a felt tip pen, which can then be wiped off with a damp cloth. The great advantage of these is that they can be used over and over again and mistakes are soon erased. They are very useful for those teachers who do not have access to a black or white board, but have the added advantage of being movable. You could produce a variety of lengths or sizes of cards, according to whether they are to have phonemic symbols, parts of words (*-ing*, *-ed*, etc.) or whole words written on them. You may choose to have a selection of colours, perhaps to highlight parts of speech (e.g. blue for nouns, red for verbs). The laminates can be used over and over again, saving money and paper and making it easy to provide materials for individual students on the spot. As mistakes are easily erased, laminates are useful for rough work, with the final draft being committed to paper. In this book, they are referred to as laminates.

Speaking

Something to talk about

The cards can be used to promote fluency. The teacher presents a selection of cards, on each of which is written a topic title – *my family, my last holiday, my ambitions, my ideal home* and so on. (See Resources and Ideas Bank.) A mixture of subjects is a good idea, so that the student can choose those which appeal. Someone with an unhappy homelife may not wish to talk about his family, while another person will feel happiest talking about this. The exercise may take the form of a monologue or a dialogue. The topic cards can be used for diagnostic purposes in the first lesson, so that the teacher would either record the student on tape to listen to later or make notes of errors of accuracy, sounds, stress and intonation. From these, part of a course could be formed.

Sample Activity Sequence A

Aim: to provide the student with practice in spoken fluency.

1 The cards are placed face down in a pile on the table.
2 The teacher turns over the top card and talks about the subject written on it.
3 The teacher places the card at the bottom of the pile when she has finished speaking.
4 The student turns over the next card and talks about the subject.
5 He places the card at the bottom of the pile when he has finished speaking.
6 The activity continues with the teacher and student alternating for as long as is effective. An odd number of cards is required so that the two will have talked about different topics each time the pile is exhausted.

Options

- When the pile has been exhausted once and the first card reappears, the student recalls what he can of what the teacher said, then speaks on the subject himself. With the second card, the teacher recalls what the student said and the activity continues in this way.

- The teacher has noted good English phrases, expressions, sentences and those containing errors. She shows the student the list and he identifies those which are correct and those which are incorrect and is guided to correct the latter.

- The student is asked to choose a specific number of cards before speaking. A shy student might feel more secure knowing how much is expected of him.

- The teacher places the cards face up on the table and invites the student to choose a subject to talk about. The teacher listens, making a note of errors of accuracy, pronunciation, stress and intonation. These errors will give the teacher an idea of the areas in which the student needs practice.

- The student is recorded on to tape and afterwards replays it, stopping the tape when he hears a mistake. (See Unit 5, Reformulation).

- As an alternative to the above, the teacher reformulates errors of phonology – pronunciation, stress, intonation – or those to do with degrees of formality.

- The student talks about the subject on the card in conjunction with Cuisenaire rods. (See Unit 7, Cuisenaire Rods.)

Tell me about this person

Here, laminates are used. Again, fluency is one aim but in this sequence of activities, there is also some work towards accuracy.

Sample Activity Sequence B

Aim: to provide practice in spoken fluency; to work on accuracy of spoken language.

1   The teacher writes the name of a person she knows on a laminate and, with the student, establishes the kinds of questions that can be asked:

What is your relationship with this person? How long have you known him?

The student writes a list of questions alone or with the teacher's help.

2   The teacher writes the names of other people she knows on individual laminates, and then invites the student to ask her about one of the people.

   Choose one of these names and ask me about the person.

3   The teacher answers the student's questions.

4   The student summarizes what the teacher has said.

5   The teacher asks the student to write the names of people he knows on some laminates.

6   The teacher asks questions about the person and the student responds.

7   The teacher summarizes what the student has said.

8   The student writes down what he has said and dictates it to the teacher.

9   The teacher corrects inaccuracies as she writes.

10 The two versions are compared.

11 The sequence can be repeated with another set of names.

Options

- The student is not given time to prepare a list of questions but asks spontaneously.
- The student provides a written version of what he has said about the people he knows.
- The word on the laminate is not the name of a person but, for example, a place, a type of food, a job, a hobby or a possession.
- If speaking about a number of people, the teacher turns each laminate face down as the person has been described. After all the people have been described and all the laminates have been turned over, the teacher repeats what has been said and the student tries to identify which of the overturned laminates carries the name of the person being described. Alternatively, the student recalls as much as he can of what the teacher said about each person and the teacher turns over the laminate which she thinks carries the name of the person being described. The teacher and student change roles.

Phonology

Minimal pairs

Students often have difficulty differentiating between and producing particular sounds. (See Unit 7, Cuisenaire Rods.) It is useful to have the phonemic symbols on individual cards, which can be introduced whenever required. The problem here lies in the difference between /əʊ/ and /ɔ:/. Each is written on a card. The teacher prepares for this activity by writing words on cards or laminates (depending on whether or not she wants to keep them). The aim of the activity is for the student to be able to sort the words into two groups, according to the minimal pairs. He is exposed to the sounds and words before being asked to say them.

Options

- At stage 8, the listener points to the phoneme on the card rather than the whole word. If the student mispronounces the word and the teacher is unable to identify it, the teacher points to a blank card. The student tries again.

Sample Activity Sequence C

Aim: to practise distinguishing between and pronouncing minimal pairs.

1 The teacher indicates two cards, on one of which is written /əʊ/ and on the other /ɔ:/. The teacher says both and the student identifies which phoneme represents which sound.
2 The teacher says the sounds again and the student repeats them.
3 The teacher gives the student a number of laminates/cards on each of which she has previously written a one-syllable word which contains the phonemes in question:
    coat, caught
    boat, bought
    sew, saw
    loan, lawn
   The teacher says each word for the student to listen to.
4 The teacher says the words again for the student to repeat.
5 The teacher involves the student in exemplification. *How do you say this word? So does it go here or here?* The teacher asks the student to sort them according to the sounds /əʊ/ and /ɔ:/.
6 The student sorts the words into two groups on his own.
7 The teacher looks at the two groups and elicits the words orally from the student one by one, confirming or correcting answers.
8 The teacher reads words from the two groups at random for the student to identify: *caught, sew, boat* and so on.
9 The roles are reversed.
10 The student copies out the two lists so that he has a written record.

Homophones

These are words which sound exactly the same but which are spelt differently and have different meanings:

wood, would
see, sea
caught, court

The aim of this activity is to help the student who has problems with sounds and spelling, as well as providing practice in using phonemic script. It is often a revelation to students that two words spelt differently have the same pronunciation, particularly if they have always said them incorrectly.

> **Sample Activity Sequence D**
>
> **Aim**: to practise spelling and pronunciation of homophones.
>
> 1 The teacher writes the homophones phonemically on laminates and asks the student to read one, e.g. /weɪ/. She asks him to write the word on another laminate:
>   *How do you spell it?*
>   He may realize that there are two ways or may need nudging:
>   *Do you know a different way?*
> 2 Having ensured that the student knows what to do, the teacher leaves him to write the rest of the homophones.
> 3 The student is asked to read out all the words he has written, being careful not to change the pronunciation of two words which should sound the same.
> 4 The student writes sentences containing the homophones to show that he understands the difference in meaning.

Options
- Instead of writing his own sentences in stage 4, the student completes a ready written gap-fill exercise.

Morphemes

These are the smallest parts of words which change meaning:

-ing (walk + ing = walking)
-ed (walk + ed = walked)
-s (walk + s = walks)

While the letters are often the same, the sounds can be different:

walks, moves, washes (/s/, /z/, /ɪz/) in the present simple.

The activity sequence overleaf revises the three different sounds of *-ed* in the past simple, which many learners pronounce in the same way – /id/. The /d/ sound follows voiced consonants such as *loved,* /t/ follows an unvoiced consonant, for example, *laughed* and /ɪd/ usually follows either /d/ or /t/.

Sample Activity Sequence E

Aim: to present and practise the pronunciation of *-ed* endings of regular verbs in the past simple.

1 The teacher places a number of laminates on the table. On each, she has written a regular verb in the infinitive. There is a mixture, according to the sound of the regular past *-ed* ending:
   walk /t/
   love /d/
   decide /ɪd/.
   She elicits the past forms from the student, who writes *-ed* on the end of each infinitive (or *ied* in some cases, such as *study*).

2 The teacher reads the verbs for the student to listen to.

3 The teacher reads them again for the student to repeat. The teacher asks: *Are they all the same?*

4 The teacher introduces three cards, on each of which is the phoneme representing one sound of the *-ed* ending:
   /d/, /t/, /ɪd/.

5 The teacher reads each sound for the student to listen to.

6 The teacher says them again for the student to repeat.

7 The teacher involves the student in exemplifying the task and then asks him to sort the verbs into three groups, according to the *-ed* sounds.

8 The student tries this on his own.

9 The teacher asks him to read them aloud and either confirms his answers or encourages him to think again. If necessary, the teacher provides a spoken model.

10 The teacher elicits the reason for the different sounds of the *-ed* ending or guides the student towards this by encouraging him to notice the final sounds of the infinitive verb forms.

11 The student puts the verbs into sentences (orally or written) and practises saying the verbs in context.

Options

- Laminates are used here so that the teacher can choose verbs for the student in question, but, of course, a permanent selection could be written on cards.

Word stress

For the student who finds stressing certain words correctly a problem, splitting words into their syllables can help.

> **Sample Activity Sequence F**
>
> **Aim**: to practise word stress.
>
> 1 The teacher writes out words whose stress the student has found difficult to remember, e.g. *photographer, banana, character.*
> 2 The teacher reads each word for the student to repeat and asks him to identify the number of syllables in one of the words, e.g. *character.*
> 3 Three laminates represent the three syllables of the word. The teacher asks the student to identify the stressed syllable and to turn the corresponding laminate (i.e. the first one) on its side, so that it stands out from the other two.
> 4 The student writes each syllable on the corresponding laminate.
> 5 The student follows the same procedure for the remaining words.
> 6 The student reads each word and records them on to tape.

Options

- The student writes each word on one laminate, but marks the stressed syllable with a different coloured pen.
- A different coloured laminate is used for the stressed syllable.
- In the case of words such as *chocolate, vegetable, comfortable* and *interesting*, which appear to have more syllables than are actually pronounced, a different approach is called for. At stage 3, the student writes the silent syllable on a laminate. He removes it before pronouncing the word – the physical removal of the laminate reflecting the need not to say it.
- A similar approach can be adopted for sentence stress.

Vocabulary

Ranking

In order to review or check understanding of new vocabulary, the student ranks words, e.g. a list of jobs, according to his opinion:

I think a farmer is a more important job than a waiter because ...

Alternatively, the criteria for this order is fixed, as in clines:

skinny, thin, plump, fat, obese.

Sample Activity Sequence G

Aim: to clarify the meaning of and practise adverbs of frequency.

1 The laminates are scattered at random on the table. Each has a frequency adverb written on it:

always	*usually*
often	*sometimes*
occasionally	*hardly ever/rarely*
never	

Also on laminates are the following percentages: *100%, 90%, 70%, 40%, 20%, 5%, 0%.*

2 The teacher models the pronunciation of each word for the student to repeat.

3 The teacher matches one of the adverbs to a percentage – such as *always = 100%* – and asks the student to match the remaining adverbs and percentages.

4 The teacher elicits the pronunciation of the words.

5 Using prompts, also written on laminates, the teacher asks questions to elicit the adverbs:

How often do you buy an English newspaper/
go swimming/travel by bus/buy chocolate/
telephone your family/send e-mails/play football?

6 The student replies using the adverbs alone or in full sentences.

7 The student uses the prompts to ask the teacher the same questions.

Options

- The questions are personalized, so that a musician, for example, is asked:

  How often do you practise/have a lesson/perform?

- Words ranked according to the student's opinion could lead to a fluency activity. For example, having ranked job titles according to ideal earnings, the student gives his reasons:

    As far as I'm concerned, a cleaner should be paid a higher salary than a secretary because ...

- Other ideas for ranking activities include:

    food – *healthiness, cost, popularity*

    sports – *popularity, cost, risk to health*

    crimes – *seriousness, type of punishment*

    reasons for going to school – *to prepare for exams, to learn social skills, to stay out of trouble.*

- Ranking a long list of words may be very difficult and could become tedious. A way round this is to ask the student to choose the top three and the bottom one.

- Other exmples of clines include:

    heat – *freezing, cold, cool, warm, hot, boiling*

    anger – *annoyed, cross/angry, furious, livid, incandescent*

    difficulty – *easy, difficult/hard, impossible*

    praise – *fair, good, excellent*

    beauty – *pretty, beautiful, stunning*

- Idioms and/or collocations can be ranked as above:

    difficulty – *a piece of cake, just about do-able, well nigh impossible*

Matching

As a way of consolidating the meaning of new vocabulary or of reviewing it, the student sorts the words into pairs according to given criteria. This may be male and female members of the family (*aunt, uncle; sister, brother*). It may be according to parts of speech, with the student grouping nouns, verbs, adjectives and so on.

Options

- The teacher dictates half the words to be reviewed, which the student writes onto laminates. He then comes up with the antonyms, which he writes on laminates of a different colour.

- The teacher provides adjectives on laminates and dictates the synonyms or antonyms of these, which the student writes on other laminates and then matches with the adjectives given.

Sorting

As a way of reviewing or consolidating the meanings of vocabulary, the student sorts words into categories:

sport – *popular/unpopular*
crime – *against people/against property*
food – *healthy/unhealthy*
furniture – *into rooms*

Options

- The student sorts words into columns according to whether he 'sees', 'hears' or 'feels' them. The teacher might choose to do this early on in the course, to help ascertain what kind of learner a student is. (See Unit 4, Learner Styles.)

- The student sorts the words according to what he likes and dislikes, needs and doesn't need, is likely to remember and is likely to forget.

Sequencing

The teacher provides a series of laminates or cards on each of which an instruction has been written. Together, these show a sequence of events or activities. For example:

put your seat belt on
start the ignition
put the car into first gear
release the handbrake

The student puts these in the correct order. Again, this may serve to review vocabulary or as an introduction to a lesson about cars or driving. The student may need to justify his choice, explaining, for example, why he starts the car before putting on a seatbelt.

Other ideas include:

cooking – *sieve the flour, add the butter, rub the flour and butter together*
using a machine – *open the lid of the photocopier, place the document to be copied face down on the glass, select the number of copies required*
travelling – *check your luggage in, wait in the departure lounge, board the plane*

Defining words

This is another way of revising vocabulary. It could be a five minute filler, used from time to time, or could form the basis of a longer activity.

Sample Activity Sequence H

Aim: to review the meanings of vocabulary.

1 The teacher prepares for this by writing words to be revised on laminates. She places these on a pile face down on the table, takes one off the top and, careful not to let the student see what is written, gives an oral definition of the word (including part of speech).

   The student says the word. If he cannot remember, the teacher gives him a clue, such as the first letter, or 'da da dums' the number of syllables and stress. The teacher shows the student the word when he has guessed it or been told.

2 The student now takes the next word and defines it for the teacher.

3 They continue to take turns until all the words have been defined.

4 The teacher drills the student's pronunciation.

5 The student writes sentences incorporating the words to show that he can use them in an appropriate context.

Options

- The first stage is as above, but instead of saying the word, the student writes it on a laminate. His version is compared with the teacher's. This will also draw attention to any spelling difficulties.

- The student matches the words to their definitions (taken from a learner's dictionary).

- If an odd number of cards is used, the activity can be repeated again once the pack has been exhausted. This will mean that the student and teacher will be working with different cards the second time.

Missing words

Here, the teacher writes out sentences on laminates in advance of the lesson. A gap is left for the student's laminate. The teacher chooses an area of lexis which the student needs to practise.

Sample Activity Sequence I

Aim: to practise appropriate use of adjectives.

1   The teacher lays out the laminates making up sentences on the table. There is a blank laminate in each sentence:
    The Taj Mahal is ... .
2   The teacher elicits a suitable adjective for the first sentence and the student writes it on the laminate.
3   The student completes the other sentences alone.
4   The student reads the completed sentences to the teacher, who discusses why words are inappropriate if necessary.

Options

*   The student writes a number of adjectives and their suitablity is discussed afterwards:
    The Taj Mahal is wonderful/magnificent/enormous.
*   Getting the student to fill in a gap helps the teacher understand his concept of the lexis. Other ideas for this type of activity include:
    parts of speech – nouns, verbs, adjectives
    word families, such as *economy, economist, economics, economical*
    degrees of formality, such as *ladies'/loo*
    spelling
*   The teacher provides three or four words for the student to choose from for each sentence. Only one is right. At higher levels, these can be very similar in meaning:
    I ... up my hand to ask the teacher a question.
    Answers: a) *rose*; b) *raised*; c) *put*. (Correct answer: *put*)
    Exam coursebooks are a useful resource for this activity.
*   The teacher provides three or four words for each sentence. Only one is wrong and the student has to identify it and justify his choice:
    It's a ... fierce dog.
    Answers: a) *very*; b) *quite*; c) *rather*. (Correct answer: *quite*)

- The teacher provides the words which complete each sentence, placing the laminates with these on to one side. The student matches the words to their sentences.
- The teacher does not leave a physical gap in the sentence, but tells the student that there is a word missing and that he should fit one in:

  My mother is housewife. (Missing word: *a*)
- The gaps review collocations:

  of *make* or *do*: *I always ... my bed after breakfast.*
  (Correct answer: *make*)

  A collocation dictionary is a useful resource.
- Grammatical components can also be practised in this way:

  possessive adjectives: *The boy cleans ... teeth.*
  (Correct answer: *his*)

Spelling

Letters written on individual cards can be a spelling aid. If the teacher does not want to spend time writing letters on small cards, an alternative is to use pieces from the boardgame 'Scrabble'.

Games

Cards, of course, lend themselves to games. Traditional games can easily be adapted for language teaching and even tailor-made for individual students.

While a certain amount of preparation is involved, the cards may be used over and over again.

Spelling games

The letters of the alphabet are written on individual cards. Here is a suggestion for how many you need of each:

E – 10	A – 7
O & U – 5	I – 4
N & R – 5	D, L, M, S & T – 4
C, G & H – 3	B, F, J, K, P, Q, V, W & Y – 2
X & Z – 1	

The idea of the game is to build up words as cards are turned over and the letters on them revealed. While it might seem unfair to pit a learner against a proficient speaker, who is likely to spot potential words first, without the element of competition, there would be little satisfaction in playing. It would be a more satisfying game for students of higher levels who enjoy playing with words.

Rules

1 The cards are spread out face down on the table.
2 The teacher and student take it in turns to turn over the cards one at a time.
3 When either of them sees that some of the letters form a word, that person takes the necessary cards and forms the word.
4 Having formed a word, that person has the next turn.
5 The game continues in this way until all the letters have been used – if possible. The winner is the person with the most words or most letters used.

Options

• The student is provided with a selection of letters and asked to produce as many words as he can from those letters. Being able to move the letters around makes this easier for some learners than pencil and paper anagrams. He keeps a written record of each word.

• The game can be made more competitive and interesting by incorporating new letters into words which have already been made (by either player) to make new words.

• A version of 'Scrabble' can also be played with the cards.

- The student forms words in response to a written phonemic version, such as /meɪl/, mail; /wɪmɪn/, women; /laɪvz/, lives.
- Also included are blank cards, which could represent any letter.

Matching games

These traditional games have many applications in language teaching. Here is a suggestion for consolidating or reviewing irregular past verb forms, playing 'memories' (or 'Pelmanism'). The teacher prepares by writing infinitive verb forms on cards of one colour and their past simple forms on cards of another colour. The different colours make for a more successful game, as the student knows whether he is picking up an infinitive or a past form. If it is difficult to get hold of different coloured card, there needs to be some other way of identifying which are present and which past forms, for example a symbol on the back of each card. This is 'fairer' as a game between unequal partners, as it depends more on memory than on a facility with language.

Rules

1 The cards are scattered over the table, face down. The teacher goes first, picking up a card of each colour and showing them to the student. If they are a match – the infinitive and its past simple form – the teacher keeps them. If not, the teacher replaces them where they were, face down, indicating that the student should remember where they are.

2 They take turns doing this. The person finding a match has the next turn.

3 The winner is the person with the most pairs of words.

Options

- The same cards can be used to play 'snap'. Of course, the words or phonemic symbols on each card will not be identical, but will match in some way. Ideas for such games include words and their phonemic versions; synonyms and antonyms; infinitives and past participles; collocations:

    have a rest, do an exam, get a letter.

Grammar

Sentence building

The aim of the following activity is to help the student who finds it difficult to recognize parts of speech.

Sample Activity Sequence J

Aim: to practise recognising parts of speech.

1 The teacher assembles a number of laminates of a variety of colours, each to be used for a different part of speech, e.g. red for nouns, green for verbs, blue for adjectives and so on.

2 The teacher writes a simple sentence on a piece of paper or laminate:

The boy played.

and shows it to the student.

3 The teacher elicits the parts of speech of each word (i.e. article, noun, verb) and asks the student to write each word on a coloured laminate of his choosing, therefore establishing that each part of speech is represented by a particular colour. This colour coding may be referred to again, so it is important that the student chooses the colours that make sense to him.

4 The teacher elicits ways of making the sentence more descriptive. *Tell me about the boy.* The student says, for example, *happy*, so the teacher indicates that he should write it on a laminate and put it into the sentence in the appropriate place: *The happy boy played.*

5 The teacher continues to elicit further information, so that the sentence grows and different parts of speech are introduced.

Options

• The exercise is limited to practise one part of speech only:
  adverbs – *The boy played quietly/happily/loudly.*

• At stage 4, the student offers *happy* and the teacher asks whether this relates to the boy or the way he played. If the former, the sentence will be *The happy boy played.* If the latter, the teacher can introduce the difference between adjectives and adverbs:

  The boy played happily.

• The exercise becomes a game, with the teacher and student taking turns to add a word at a time, to see how long a sentence they can make.

- The student is presented with an incomplete sentence (see **Vocabulary**): *The boy played …* and finishes it in as many ways as he can:

  The boy played happily.
  The boy played in the garden.
  The boy played every day.
  The boy played cricket with his brother.
  The boy played a trick on his brother.
  The boy played the guitar.
  The boy played records very loudly.
  The boy played truant from school.

- The sentence is long to begin with and reduced by one or two words at a time, with each version a full sentence:

  I'd love to go out dancing with you on Saturday night.
  I'd love to go dancing with you on Saturday night.
  I'd love to go dancing with you on Saturday.
  I'd love to go dancing with you.
  I love to go dancing with you.
  I love dancing with you.
  I love dancing.

Word order

English word order is very different from that of some other languages, and is, consequently, a problem for many learners, who may come up with sentences such as *He speaks very well French*. They may be helped by physically moving around parts of a sentence or by the use of different coloured laminates to help them notice patterns of colour – and, therefore perhaps, of grammar – within sentences.

Sample Activity Sequence K

Aim: to practise word order with time expressions.

1 The teacher shows the student three or four sentences which include time expressions, such as *Shane sends e-mails twice a week*. The teacher encourages the student to notice the position of the time expression.

2 The teacher provides the student with a number of laminates, on each of which are written words of a sentence, such as *every/Geoff/to/drove/day/London*. The teacher asks the student to put them in the correct order.

3 The student does so, referring to the examples if necessary.

4 Once the correct order has been established, the student writes the sentences down, so that he has a written record to refer to.

Options

- The teacher provides the student with the words of sentences on laminates and reads out each sentence once. The student arranges the laminates in the right order. This encourages listening and may help students notice language patterns aurally.

Word pools

These are groups of words which are placed within some kind of framework, for example a hoop or piece of string arranged in a ring. They provide words with which the student can make a number of sentences in order to practise a particular aspect of language.

Sample Activity Sequence L

Aim: to practise forming negatives and questions in the present simple.

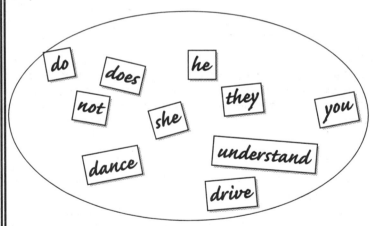

1 The teacher prepares a number of laminates, each with one word written on as in the picture.
2 The teacher places the laminates in the 'pool', takes out one of the words and places it in front of her, explaining that she is going to make a sentence and inviting the student to help.
3 The student forms as many words as he can, writing each one down before returning the laminates to the pool and beginning a new sentence.

Options

- The different parts of speech are written on different coloured cards to ease identification.
- The same laminates are used to create a substitution table:

Do ⎱ you ⎱ smoke
⎰ they ⎱ understand
⎱ drive
Does he/she ⎰ dance

Using a text

Laminates can be used along with a text to help develop the student's reading skills. The first activity aims to give practice in predicting the content of a text and, if further work is to be done on it, gives him a non-threatening introduction to the text. The whole exercise may have more meaning for the student if he has chosen the text. (This can be done at any time beforehand to give the teacher the chance to look at the text).

Sample Activity Sequence M

Aim: to predict the content of a text.

1 The student is shown the title or headline of the text and the accompanying picture if there is one.
2 He writes on laminates any words he predicts will be in the text.
3 He scans it to see if any of those words are there.

Options

- The student explains why he thinks the predicted words will be in the text.
- This can be done provided enough of the student's words appear in the text. Having finished scanning, the student discards those words which did not appear and predicts the significance of the remaining words. The student then reads the text intensively to see if he was right.
- The teacher provides a number of words which appear in the text and the student asks 'yes/no' questions about their relevance, e.g. *appalling – is this word used to describe the living conditions?*
- The teacher provides a list of words which occur in the text and the student puts them in the order in which he thinks

they appear. To follow on from this, he builds up an idea of the text orally.

- The student uses the successfully predicted key words to retell the text after reading it.
- The teacher provides the words for prediction – some are in the text and some are not.

Sequencing

Here is another way of predicting the content of a text, this time encouraging the student to skim read.

Sample Activity Sequence N

Aim: to practise skimming a text.

1 The teacher gives the student a number of laminates on each of which has been written the gist of one of the paragraphs in the text:

    the house where he was born
    the house where he lives now
    his favourite room when he was a child
    the type of house he would like.

2 The student puts them in the order in which he thinks they will appear.

3 The student skim reads the text to find out if he is right. If not, he rearranges the laminates to show the correct order.

Options

- This is practical only for short texts. The teacher writes the sentences of the entire text on laminates and the student puts them in a predicted order, then checks against the original. This could be used to introduce the student to linking words, such as *first, then, after that* or to simple reference devices such as pronouns, *this means* and *which is*.
- The student is presented with the text and key words, the latter on laminates. Within a given time limit, he scans the text in order to sort the words into groups, for example, the protagonist's life before he became famous and his life since he became famous.

09

corresponding and writing

In this unit you will learn
- about the role of writing in your student's learning
- about the use of a student diary
- how to use selective dictation to focus on language issues
- how to exploit writing to and alongside your student

Writing is sometimes treated as the poor relation of the four skills, given as homework, so as not to 'waste' classroom time, though if the teacher apparently sees it as a less valuable skill than the others, she should not be surprised if the student feels the same and does not do it. Writing may also be seen as a solo activity, which it need not be, so that the one-to-one teacher might feel awkward giving the student something to write instead of seeming to 'be teaching'.

Everybody communicates by writing sometimes, whether by hand, on a typewriter, via e-mail or on a computer. It is, therefore, a skill worth working on. There are several aspects to it: style; level of formality; tone; appropriate layout (of letters, for example); grammatical structure; vocabulary, collocations and so on.

For the student who finds speaking hard work, writing may prove a more satisfactory or less inhibiting means of communication. There is time to think before committing to paper and the chance to correct or redraft before showing anyone. Some students excel at writing, while their oral communication skills are less impressive; giving them the opportunity to write gives them the chance to shine. Furthermore, as the student has time to consider before writing, any areas where he is having problems will be highlighted, so that writing also has a diagnostic purpose, and the teacher will find referring to the student's written work helpful when designing the syllabus. For example, if the piece contains several errors relating to word order, the teacher could incorporate work on word order into the syllabus.

The student writing alone

Diaries

For the student used to writing a diary in his native tongue, this is a natural extension of that activity. For those unused to doing so, keeping a diary may be seen as something special to do while away from home (or simply in a different environment if that is not the case). It serves as a record of the time spent studying, whether abroad or not, and may become part of the retrospective course-book. (See Unit 6, Coursebooks, Retrospective Coursebooks and Blank Tapes.) The teacher can introduce the idea early on in the course and discuss with the student how to approach it.

The first option is for the student to keep the diary private. It may be the first time he has written in English purely for himself and a diary is, for most of us, something personal and not done for the general public. Mistakes will remain undiscovered, feelings private, which is liberating.

Alternatively, the teacher may explain in advance that she will be reading either excerpts selected by the student or all of the diary. How much the teacher will see could be decided by both. By way of correcting, the teacher and student could take turns to reformulate the selected passages in writing. (See Unit 5, Reformulation.)

Dictation

While the student is practising writing, dictation cannot, of course, be separated from the skill of listening. Writing exactly what the teacher reads out is only one way of doing a dictation. The length of text may be according to level, but it does not necessarily follow that advanced students like long dictations! Isolated sentences can be dictated, too.

One can read relatively slowly and very clearly without resorting to being unnatural. If the idea is to accustom the student to the sound of English, it is helpful to speak with natural connections between words, rather than saying each one in isolation. With a student who has great difficulty hearing English, however, the line or sentence could be read as normal first, then reread with each word being carefully enunciated, before being repeated as normal again.

This is an example of a dictation which has been designed for a speaker of a specific language. Japanese, Russian and Turkish, among others, are languages which do not contain articles, so their use in English can be confusing. Other languages, such as French and Portuguese, have articles, but sometimes use them differently. The following errors were made by a Japanese student:

My mother is teacher.
first time I went by plane.
I love UK, but I don't like cold.
I used to catch a snake.

It may be that the student is not even hearing articles and this dictation will show whether or not this is the case. It is better if the teacher does not warn the student what she is focusing on, as this could add undue pressure. However, afterwards, the teacher could explain that she is only looking for errors related to articles and will ignore other mistakes. Alternatively, the teacher could respond to all the errors, but paying particular attention to article-related mistakes with a view to including work on articles in the syllabus.

Sample Activity Sequence A

Aim: to provide practice in listening for articles.

1 The teacher chooses or writes a text of a few sentences which contains a number of definite and/or indefinite articles (according to which she wishes to practise).
2 The teacher sets the student a listening task, such as a question about the gist, and then reads the text. The student gives the answer orally.
3 The teacher explains that she will read short phrases, repeating each once or twice before moving on and that the student should write exactly what he hears. (The articles might be at the beginning, end or in the middle of the phrase.)
4 The teacher rereads the whole text, so that the student can listen and follow what he has written.
5 The teacher and student compare the latter's text with the original.

Options

• The teacher records the dictation for the student to do for homework.
• The teacher rereads each phrase as often as the student requests it.
• Instead of comparing his own text with the original, the student dictates what he has written back to the teacher. Where he has omitted an article, the teacher rereads the relevant phrase for him to find out if he can hear it.
• After dictating the text, the teacher checks the student's version. If articles are missing, she asks if the student can think of anything which might be missing from his version and

rereads the text in short phrases. If the student is still not hearing the articles, the teacher points out that those are what are missing from his version and rereads the text in the same phrases as before.

- The same procedure can be used for other language items, not necessarily according to the student's mother tongue and L1 interference (see Glossary). Other ideas include regular past tenses; 3ʳᵈ person 's'; numbers (*40; 14*).

- The text contains a number of examples of a sound which the student has difficulty hearing and pronouncing. The dictation provides further exposure to the sound(s), e.g. *court, caught, bought, saw*, which contain the sound /ɔ:/. The passage could also contain minimal pairs, e.g. *ran, run; sang, sung; cat, cut*. It may be an opportunity for the student to practise looking at the context of the word in order to work out its most likely meaning and spelling:

    The children ran to school every day last summer.

    The last two words make it clear that only *ran* (and not *run*) is possible here. The teacher could dictate *The children ran to school* initially, adding *last summer* to help the student work out the meaning from the context.

- Selective dictation: the teacher dictates a text containing several dates, with the student writing only these. Instead of dates, numbers, countries or parts of speech could be practised.

As well as the deliberate inclusion of certain language items, omission of specific items is also possible. In this case, the student fills in the missing words or phrases.

Sample Activity Sequence B

Aim: to practise passive forms.

1 The teacher chooses or writes a text or sentences which contain passive forms in whichever tense(s) the student is familiar.

2 The teacher explains that she is going to dictate everything except the auxiliaries and asks the student to include those as he writes.

3 The teacher dictates, reading each phrase twice, but omitting the auxiliaries:

    The burglar arrested last night.

4 The student writes what he hears, as well as the missing auxiliaries:

    *The burglar **was** arrested last night.*

5 The teacher and student compare the latter's version of the text with the original.

Options

- Alternatives to missing auxiliaries include:

    3rd person 's' – the teacher reads *Mr Wilson enjoy travelling.*
    The student writes *Mr Wilson enjoys travelling.*

    articles – *He's been to Mexico and USA.*
    He's been to Mexico and the USA.

    plural 's' – *Have you got any brother?*
    Have you got any brothers?

- The dictation could be used in conjunction with a picture or series of pictures making up a story, so that the student can insert the missing words, such as prepositions. The teacher shows, for example, a picture of a boy looking for something and dictates:

    The boy looked his football boots. They were the bed.

    The student writes:

    *The boy looked **for** his football boots. They were **under** the bed.*

- The student writes only what the teacher dictates in the first instance and then returns to the text to fill in the missing information, rather than doing it as he goes along. This could be used for the above sequence, but is also suitable where an overall understanding of the text is necessary in order to complete it, such as inserting missing pronouns and determiners:

    ***My** sister was born when **I** was five years old. **She** was an adorable baby. **Her** name is Catherine.*

    The teacher could make a little noise or tap on the table if it is necessary to point out the gaps.

- The teacher dictates the passage, occasionally inserting a word which is the wrong part of speech. The student writes it in the correct form.

    *The cost of the machine was (prohibition) **prohibitive**, so we didn't buy it.*

- Some students might be unsure about when to use capital letters, particularly those who speak a language with a different script, such as Arabic and Chinese or one where capital letters are not used as they are in English, such as French (*Monday* translates as *lundi* but is not written with a capital initial). The teacher dictates a text or sentences which contain a number of capital letters, such as initial letters for days of the week, nationalities and so on. The student judges when capital letters should be used. The use of punctuation marks can be practised in the same way.

Authentic writing

Here, the student writes 'for real'. Before the course begins, he may have written or e-mailed for information, in some cases directly to the teacher. This gives an idea of his level.

The student may be encouraged to send postcards and letters of thanks written in English to English speakers.

Writing, as has been mentioned, is not necessarily a skill which needs to be done alone. It can be a collaboration between the teacher and student. Even if it is done alone, some kind of response will be required. Writing is usually transactional – invitations and job application letters receive replies; cheques are 'exchanged' for goods. As with other skills work, the student needs to know why he is being asked to carry out a certain task.

Collaborative texts

Consequences

Instead of writing alone, the student can work with the teacher. A game like 'consequences' works well, because it involves a minimum of writing and cannot be played by just one person. It is also the simplest form of narrative and a gentle introduction to the art. The following is an activity sequence for a more involved narrative.

Sample Activity Sequence C

Aim: to practise narrative building.

1 The teacher and student each have a piece of paper. Each begins writing a story. The theme may be inspired, for example, by pictures, a past or forthcoming event or a title chosen by one for the other.
2 After an agreed period of time, say five minutes, or after writing one sentence, they exchange pieces of paper and continue the story they now have in front of them.
3 The activity continues in this way until both stories are finished. It is advisable to decide in advance how many times the stories are to be exchanged.
4 Both parties read the stories silently and then comment as appropriate.
5 They work on correction. (See **Correction** section below.)

Options

- There is only one narrative between the two, the student and teacher writing alternate sentences.
- There are three narratives on the go!
- Alternatives to stories include letters, accounts, references, reviews – perhaps of differing opinions of the same show/book/film.
- The teacher and student adopt different roles and write 'in character'. One idea is to write about the same subject from a different viewpoint. For example, there could be a boxer and a doctor arguing *for* and *against* boxing, with the student and teacher writing as each character alternately.
- One piece is written in the first person singular and one in the third person singular. Alternatively, different tenses are practised; in one the past is used and in the other, the present.
- Both pieces contain the same information but are written with different target readers in mind. For example, a letter giving directions to a meeting – one to a close friend and the other to an important guest speaker – could be written at two levels of formality.
- Certain words have to be included. These could be irregular verbs, recently presented vocabulary or whatever needs to be practised.
- The student and teacher have a written 'conversation', with neither speaking, but writing instead. This allows time for reflection, so need not be hurried. It may be topic based or just a chat.

Chat room

This technique is based on Internet communication. The teacher writes her name on the left hand side of the paper and initiates a written conversation. The student writes his name below and replies. The conversation continues in silence. It could be used to incorporate a function, such as inviting, asking for help, thanking. An option is for each person to take on an extra role, so that four people are involved in the conversation. In effect, the teacher and student are now involved in role play.

Correction

As with spoken errors, written errors can be corrected immediately or retrospectively. There is more on immediate correction in Unit 5, Reformulation.

The teacher may choose to decide in advance on the criteria for correction, particularly if she predicts that there will be many errors. It is disheartening for students who lack confidence to get back a piece of work which has been obliterated by the teacher's corrections. The criteria for correction could be agreed on beforehand, so that the student is focusing on one particular area of language, be it grammar, spelling, appropriacy of vocabulary, while writing. For example, the student may be having difficulty with the use of the past perfect, so he has been asked to write a narrative and the teacher and student agree that the former will focus on the use of the past perfect when correcting the script.

Sample correction

Here is an example of a written error, followed by a variety of ways of correcting it:

The student has written: *I must to do my homework this afternoon.*

Teacher   *What kind of word is 'must'?*
Student   *A modal verb.*
Teacher   *What always comes after a modal?*
Student   *An infinitive.*
Teacher   *Do we need 'to'?*
Student   *No.*

If the teacher chooses not to discuss the corrections, written comments in the margin will jog the student's memory. For this reason, it is a good idea for the student to write on every other line. The teacher locates the error by underlining it and guides the student towards categorizing it. It is also a good idea for the student to write on alternate lines so that there is room for the teacher to write comments.

The student has written: *I must to do my homework this afternoon.*

The teacher writes in the student's absence: *What kind of word is this? What follows it?*

Alternatively, the comments can be recorded on to tape for the student to listen to alone while he is rereading the piece of writing.

Correction codes

Another idea is to categorize errors by means of a code. For example:

Grammar – **gr**   Word order – **wo**
Punctuation – **punct**   Preposition – **prep**
Spelling – **sp**   Article – **art**
Tense – **t**   Wrong Word – **ww**
Vocabulary (i.e. inappropriacy) – **v**   Verb problem – **vb**

The errors are underlined and the relevant category initials written in the margin. Thus:

gr   *I must <u>to</u> do my homework this afternoon.*

Example of written work marked with correction code

This is an extract from a letter written by a student to his teacher.

<u>Had you</u> a stressful time in your job <u>on</u> January?
gr   *prep*

I think many new students arrived <u>in</u>
                   prep

<u>this time at school</u>.
w.o.

Your friend <u>lifes now</u> in Australia,
     v & w.o.

do you <u>want visite</u> him in the future?
      gr & sp

I've been learning 'salsa' <u>dance</u> in the <u>next</u> few weeks.
              v   *v*

I like <u>dance</u> this very <u>well</u>.
     gr   *gr*

Yesterday, I went with Monica from our school

in London by 'Madam Tussaud's' and in
　　　w.o.   prep　　　　　　　　　　　*prep*

the 'Planetarium'. <u>We've seen</u> a lot of famous
　　　　　　　　　　　t

people in wax and <u>I've taken</u> many
　　　　　　　　t

photos. In my <u>opionion</u>, most of <u>them</u>
　　　　　　　　　sp　　　　　　*gr*

faces are so real.

Colour coding

Coloured pens or pencils are an alternative way of coding errors. A colour coding system could be used (e.g. red for verbs, blue for word order, green for spelling) so that it is easy to see in which area the student has most difficulties.

Errors log

It is useful for the student to keep a record of the kinds of mistakes he makes.

	articles	prepositions	spelling	past tenses
script 1	8	5	12	8
script 2	6	6	9	5
script 3	4	7	8	2

In this way, the student keeps a log of progress.

If a number of the same kind of mistakes occurs, it is likely that the student does not understand the language point. In addition to the above errors, the following also appears in the piece of writing:

I can't to go out tonight because I have to call my parents. I will to arrange my birthday.

It is clear that the student is having difficulty with the form of modals within a sentence. Rather than marking each error separately, the teacher could asterisk these and write correction comments at the end of the piece. It is highly likely that she will review modals with the student. Errors, then, are not just 'bad'.

They serve a diagnostic purpose, which the teacher will find very useful.

The student can also be encouraged to correct his own work – something which is difficult to do. There are too many things to consider, so the teacher can help by narrowing the choice. Having read the piece but not marked it, the teacher asks the student to go through it looking for specific items. In the above case, for example, she might say:

Teacher   *I want you to read your letter and underline all the modal verbs.*
          (The student does so.) *Now look at the words which come after these.*

Or
Teacher   *What do you know about modals?*
Student   *They are not real verbs. They have an infinitive after them.*
Teacher   *What do you know about the infinitive?*
Student   *No 'to'.*
Teacher   *Good. Now, I want you to read your letter again. Look at all the modals and see what comes after them.*

Less specifically, the teacher might suggest the student checks the modal verbs in his piece of writing. Because there are so many areas where things can go wrong, it is helpful for the student to read through his writing, looking at language items by category, particularly those which are 'weak points', such as no 3rd person 's', plural adjectives, word order of adverbs of frequency, and inconsistencies in degrees of formality.

It is important to praise as well as to criticize. Appropriate language, carefully organized ideas, well-crafted sentences need to be recognized. Effective communication of ideas in spite of errors can also receive positive feedback. Positive comments will boost the student's morale.

Student–teacher correspondence

Letter writing is a purposeful task and what is particularly motivating for the student is the certain knowledge that the content of his letter will be acknowledged in the teacher's reply, rather than just the form.

There are two approaches to correction here. Apart from the methods described above, there is the following option. The student's letter is not returned with the teacher's writing all over it, rather it remains as it was when he sent it. Accompanying the teacher's reply is the original letter and a reformulated version. By comparing the two, perhaps the student will think about his mistakes. This does, however, depend on the kind of learner he is. (See Unit 4, Learner Styles.)

The teacher writes the first letter, pitching it at the same level as or slightly above the student's. In it she introduces herself, as you would in the first letter to a penfriend. The teacher includes one or two questions or invitations to write about a particular subject to encourage the student in his reply. Between them, they may decide on the frequency of the letters, perhaps one a week or, in the case of a short course, a few words every day.

Corresponding with a Japanese student

Here is the first letter written to a Japanese student at pre-intermediate level who had been in England for several weeks but who was having difficulty understanding spoken English and for whom speaking often seemed something of an ordeal:

Dear Shuhei,

I am writing to tell you something about myself.

I am 38 and single. I have two brothers and a sister, who are all younger than me. One of my brothers got married last summer. His wife is very nice.

I live alone in a small flat in London. It's a great place, but I don't really like living here, so I'd like to move to the country one day. I enjoy sitting in my garden in the summer.

I teach English at a school in Bromley. I love meeting people from different countries. I've never been to Japan, so I'd be very interested to know about it.

Please write soon. I'm looking forward to reading your letter.

Best wishes

Sara

The teacher's letter serves as a model from which the student may take ideas or phrases. Here are the opening and closing lines from Shuhei's reply.

> I'm writing to tell you something about myself and my family.
>
> ---
>
> I'm looking forward to reading your letter!

Once she has received a reply, the teacher answers, also optionally producing a reformulated version of the student's letter, changing only what is wrong. For example:

> I had enjoy, but I was tired because very long time travel!

> I had a great time, but I was tired because the journey was very long!

Of course, there are different ways of reformulating and the correction could also have been: *I really enjoyed myself.* The important thing is to retain the spirit of the message and it may be relevant to consider the student's age and personality when deciding what sort of language to use.

Shuhei's last letter, however, finishes with the line:

> We were very enjoyed.

Nonetheless, over a three month period, his letters became longer, more detailed and confident. He seemed to appreciate the opportunity to express himself in his own time, without the stress of face to face communication. In response to this:

> *What are your hobbies and interests? Let me know in your next letter.*

he was bold enough to write:

> Sorry, I don't understand 'let me know'.

The teacher replied:

> *'Let me know' means 'tell me' about something. I know you went to Paris last weekend, so let me know all about it in your next letter!*

Of course this is correspondence and not interrogation! Shuhei also asked questions:

> I'm going to stay UK more 24 days. I wont to go to a lot of good place. Can you recommend a good place?

> *I'm going to stay <u>in the UK for 24 more days</u>. I w<u>a</u>nt to go to a lot of good place<u>s</u>. Can you recommend a good place?*

The teacher does not change the language which is correct. The underlined errors stand out, which means that the parts of the student's original which were correct are also easy to see. The student can see at a glance that what he has written contains more that is right than wrong. At higher levels, the grammar may be correct, but particular words or phrases inappropriate for the style, so these can be reformulated by the teacher.

Corresponding with a Chinese student

Different approaches towards encouraging correction were attempted with a pre-intermediate Chinese student.

> ...because my English isn't very well, so my father wanted me to go out our country study more things...

> My English isn't very _____, so my father wanted me to _____ our country to study more.

The student did not fill in the gaps. Following the next letter, the teacher tried a different approach:

> Alright, next time I'll tell you my childhood. By the way, if you want to know more something, please tell me. I'll very pleasure give you answer.

> _All right_, next time I'll tell you _about_ my childhood. By the way, if you want to know _anything else_, please tell me. I'll _be very pleased_ to give you _an_ answer.

She responded well to this approach:

> Thank you for your letter and revised my worried letter.

However, following this:

> Now I'd like to told you about my childhood.

> Now I'd like to _____ you about my childhood.
>   verb form

the student responded:

> By the way, next time when you repair my wrong letter,
> I'm prefer you wrote down the right words in my letter. I
> don't like you put the gap and I need put the words in.
> Thank you!

So …

> By the way, next time you <u>correct</u> my mistakes, I don't
> <u>want you to</u> put the gaps <u>so that</u> I need to put the
> words in. Thank you!

When asked in the next letter why she preferred this method of correction and whether or not she would read the corrections, she replied:

> Thank you very much you correct my mistakes. I prefer it because you correct my mistakes give me a direction impression. It's very helpful my memory. Of course I'll read them. Every time when you replyed and correct my letter it's very important for me. Every letters I used the stapler made they togeither.

While the above is not hard to understand, sometimes a student's errors make comprehension more difficult. For example:

> Do you know how many kind of the Chinese martial arts? How do you feel it's true or untrue?

So ...

> Do you know how many kind<u>s</u> of martial arts <u>there are</u>? <u>Do you believe it?</u> (I hope this is what you mean here – I'm not sure.)

Whether or not the student learned from her errors is a moot point, but the fact is she found the correspondence enjoyable and helpful and it provided her with a different means of expression.

Indeed, she became quite poetic and related stories about her homelife which the teacher had not anticipated. The student once wrote:

> ... [the letters from the teacher] because they are all give me a feeling is soft and beautiful.

Corresponding also gave her the opportunity to express how she felt about her English. The following excerpts are taken from a long paragraph in which she attacked herself for her lack of progress.

> Honestly, I do really hated I often make mistakes. I feel guilt, anxiety and embarrass... I'm robbish at English grammar, it's so difficult to me to write and speak.

What is impressive about the above, however, is the natural use of *honestly* and the emphatic *do*. For some, letter writing may prove therapeutic and, as long as the words remain unspoken, it is safe to express oneself, as if to an 'agony aunt'. This student clearly needs boosting, so the following method of correction and reformulation was adopted:

> ...I know I can do something else, but if I couldn't learned... I feel very gloomy... I loved this feeling, although you are a teacher, we are look like friend... Tidying up in the garden for someone is boring things, for example my landlord...

...I know I <u>can do</u> something else, but if I <u>couldn't learn</u> ... I
　　　　　　good - can + infin　　　　　　　　　　　　could + infin

feel very <u>gloomy</u> ... I love this feeling.
　　　good word

Although you are a teacher, we <u>are like</u> friends...Tidying up
in the garden <u>is boring for some people</u>, for example my
landlord.

This correction system make it easier to me to
understand what kind of mistakes I make.

Corresponding with a Swiss student

The following is taken from a letter written by a German speaking Swiss man at intermediate level:

...I can use the telephone from my hostfamily... Now, when I
phone to Switzerland, I use the telephone from my hostfamily.

The teacher encouraged the student to look at a correction made earlier in the letter:

...I can use <u>my host family's</u> telephone... Now, when I
phone Switzerland, I use _____ .
　　　　　　Look at the way to say this above.

Students are bound to respond differently to this approach; while some will notice their errors immediately and learn from them, for others this may be challenging, as has been shown in the examples above. However, correspondence between student and teacher is a valuable exercise, not only because it encourages the teacher to focus as much on content as on form, but also because it increases the variety of interactions between the two.

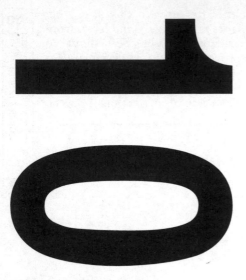

10 peopling and placing the room

In this unit you will learn
- about ways of relieving the intensity of one-to-one teaching
- about techniques to bring in virtual third parties to the study room for role play and speaking activities
- how to use real and imaginary photographs
- how to enliven the room through the use of the telephone and props

Background

One of the challenges of working with just one student is the intensity that the situation can create. One way of breaking the intensity is to bring virtual people and places into the room. In so doing, the majority of the activities in this unit engage the student in spoken or written production.

> ## Think about
>
> How could you break the intensity of the one-to-one situation by:
>
> **a** using an empty chair?
> **b** swapping roles with the student?
> **c** using a virtual photo album?
> **d** guiding the student to visualize a scene?
> **e** bringing in a real photograph?
> **f** looking at the view outside the window?
> **g** displaying postcards?
> **h** picking up a telephone?

The hot-seat

Techniques borrowed from psychodrama provide one way of peopling the room. Psychodrama includes a set of procedures used in Gestalt therapy. In the therapeutic setting, rather than *talking about* issues, the client *enacts* them. One psychodrama technique is known as 'doubling the hot-seat' or empty chair. In the therapy room, questions are addressed to an empty chair by the client, who then replies in the voice of the occupant of the seat. For example, the client may ask her absent mother questions and then reply to those questions as though she were her mother.

Doubling the hot-seat

In the study space the teacher selects a person she knows, for example, her husband, and places the name of that person on an empty chair between her and the student. The teacher should make clear what her relationship with that person is. The student asks the 'person' on the empty chair questions in the 'you' form and the teacher replies in the first person on her husband's behalf. If the teacher sits on the empty chair, it will make answering in the first person more natural. For example:

Student	*What's your job?*
Teacher (as husband)	*I'm a postman.*
Student	*Where do you work?*
Teacher (as husband)	*In Bromley ...*

In this way the face-to-face intensity of the one-to-one lesson is broken with the introduction of a virtual third party.

A variation on this activity is for the student to choose the identity of someone known to him and for the teacher to address questions to the empty chair while the student replies in the first person as the absent person.

Sample Activity Sequence A

Aim: to practise asking questions to find out personal information; to practise summarizing personal information.

1 The teacher selects a person for the empty chair, such as a friend who is unknown to the student.
2 The teacher and student work together on questions to ask the friend: *What's your name? Where do you live?* and so on.
3 The student asks the questions and the teacher replies on behalf of the absent person.
4 The student summarizes orally all the information he has found out about the absent person.

Options
• The teacher and student can target a particular topic area for the conversation, for example:

    work – *Tell me about your job.*

    holidays – *What was your best/worst/cheapest/longest, etc. holiday?*

    sport – *Tell me about the sports you like/don't like.*

See the topic list in the Resources and Ideas Bank on page 167.
• A particular time relation can be targeted, for example, all the questions must be about the past, the present, the future or general time.
• A function can be targeted, for example:

    asking about plans – *What are you doing at the weekend? What are your career plans?*

daily routines – *Describe your weekday/Sunday routine.*
instructions – *How do you use the cassette player?*
directions – *How do I get to your house from here?*

- The question and answer stage can be recorded on tape and then replayed to work on the language.
- The whole question and answer stage could be conducted in writing – the student writing the question on one line and the teacher the answer on the next. For example:

Student (writes)   *What do you usually do on Sundays?*

Teacher (writes)   *I always get up late. And then I read the Sunday papers.*

Then if necessary the student can be involved in correcting his questions at the end. Alternatively, each of the student's questions could be reformulated on the line beneath as the written conversation goes along. For example:

Student (writes in error)   *Where you going for the next holiday?*

Teacher (writes on the next line)   *Where are you going for your next holiday?*

Then the whole conversation can be practised through reading aloud with the student and teacher taking it in turns to read the questions and answers. Finally, the whole conversation can be recorded on to tape, once with the student reading the questions and the teacher the answers and then the other way round.

- The summaries by the student can be spoken, reformulated, written, and/or recorded.
- Of course, the interaction between the student and the virtual person need not remain on the level of pure question and answer. The interchange can become less artificial and follow the characteristics of an ordinary conversation. In a business lesson the exchange can model interaction with a client or colleague. In a business context the teacher and student decide on the person or their role and the goal of the interaction, for example, presenting a product, arranging a meeting.
- The questions to the occupant of the empty seat can be asked in the third person (*What's his job?*) and the answers can be given in the third person (*He works in a bank*).

Sample Activity Sequence B

Aim: to practise giving personal information.

1 The student selects a person for the empty chair (e.g. his brother).
2 The teacher asks questions and the student replies on behalf of the absent person.
3 The teacher summarizes the information she has found out.
4 The student reformulates the teacher's summary.

The occupants of the empty chair

The occupants of the empty chair can be real people known to the student or teacher – family, friends, colleagues, famous people or celebrities, or they could be role specific – bank manager, shop assistant, tourist information person. A photograph or picture of a person can be placed on the empty chair as a focus. In a business lesson the occupants of the empty chair could be job-related clients, members of the management team. Needs analysis carried out with the student is useful here (see Unit 1). Consult the list of people the student specified as interlocutors and use them as occupants of the empty chair.

Generating identities for the empty chair

Another way of peopling the room with the aid of the empty chair is for the student and teacher to decide together on the identity of an *imaginary* person, for example, a neighbour. The teacher lives on one side of the neighbour, the student lives on the other. The teacher and student ask each other questions about their common neighbour and in so doing generate an identity for them. For example:

Teacher   *Do you know his name?*
Student   *Mr Brown, I think. Do you know if he's married?*
Teacher   *He's a widower actually. He's got a daughter who visits now and then. How often do you see him?*
Student   *Well, I see him in the garden in the summer ...*

Sample Activity Sequence C

Aim: to practise asking questions and summarizing personal information.

1 The teacher and student decide on the relationship they have with an occupant of the empty chair, such as an imaginary work colleague in the student's workplace.
2 The teacher and student have five minutes to think of details they know about the occupant. The teacher can help with language if necessary.
3 The teacher and student have the conversation about the person, asking each other questions and sharing information to build up an imagined persona.
4 The student summarizes orally what he now knows about this imaginary person.
5 The teacher reformulates what the student has summarized.

Options

• Possible relationships between the triangle of teacher, student and the occupant of the empty chair include:

colleagues

doctor and local shopkeeper

daughter and neighbour

two people with opposing views of the occupant (e.g. mother of the occupant accused of a crime and the arresting officer)

two witnesses of an accident when the occupant is the driver.

• As before, the conversation can be written or spoken. The teacher can reformulate each part of the student's conversation. The conversation can be recorded for language work.

• The student's summary can be written, spoken and/or reformulated.

Role swapping

Role swapping involves the teacher and the student continually doubling each other's roles. For example, the teacher plays the role of a shop assistant in a newsagent's while the student is the customer. The role play begins:

Teacher *Can I help you?*

On a specified signal (for example, teacher and student swap role labels on cards), the teacher and student swap roles – the teacher becomes the customer and the student the shop assistant. They continue these roles for a while and then they swap roles again and so on.

This procedure maximizes involvement and builds in plenty of task repetition but without the potential tedium of simply repeating the whole role play. It also means that the student is continually re-exposed to appropriate language for both roles.

Sample Activity Sequence D

Aim: to practise making polite requests and spoken fluency.

1 Decide on the roles and the objective of the role play. For example, shop assistant and customer in a newsagent's; the customer wants to buy *The Times*, a Mars bar, and a book of first class stamps.
2 Look at possible language to be used in the role play. For example: *Can I help you? Yes, please? Can I have …?*
3 The teacher has a card with her role written on it: 'Shop Assistant', the student has his role label: 'Customer'.
4 The role play begins.
5 Sooner or later the teacher gives her role card to the student and vice versa. The role play restarts.
6 Sooner or later the teacher gives her role label to the student and vice versa and the role play begins again. And so on.

Sample role play:

Teacher (Shop Assistant)	*Can I help you?*
Student (Customer)	*The Times, please.*

(The teacher initiates the role label swap.)

Student (Shop Assistant)	*Can I help you?*
Teacher (Customer)	*Can I have The Times, please?*
Student (Shop Assistant)	*Here you are.*
Teacher (Customer)	*Thanks. And a Mars bar, please.*

Student (Shop Assistant)   *OK.*
(Teacher initiates the role label swap.)
Teacher (Shop Assistant)   *Can I help you?*
Student (Customer)   *The Times, please.*
Teacher (Shop Assistant)   *Here you are, sir.*
Student (Customer)   *And a Mars bar, please.*
Teacher (Shop Assistant)   *OK.*
Student (Customer)   *And do you have books of stamps?*
(Teacher initiates the role label swap. And so on!)

Options

- Look at useful language for the role play after running it once. Then repeat the role play.
- When swapping roles, continue the role play rather than restart it.
- Run the whole role play without swapping roles. Then re-do the role play with roles swapped.
- Consult the list of interlocutors and situations drawn up during needs analysis with the student to select roles and role play scenarios.
- The teacher can decide to swap roles and reformulate what the student has just said where this seems useful because of the student's English.
- The student initiates the role label swap.

Photographs

The virtual album

Another device for bringing other people into the room is the use of a virtual photo album. The student folds a blank sheet of paper to create an 'album'. The student thinks of, say, four real or imaginary photos from his family album and draws four empty squares or rectangles to represent the pictures. He should not draw or sketch in the content of the photos. The student describes the people in the photos, including whether the photos are black and white or colour, who took the pictures, when and why and so on. This activity clearly promotes attentive listening in order to recall the information which is not visually available.

Sample Activity Sequence E

Aim: to practise spoken fluency talking about family photos.

1 The teacher explains the activity by folding a sheet of paper and drawing the outline of each photograph in her own album.
2 The teacher describes her photos.
3 The student summarizes what he remembers of the teacher's photos.
4 The student creates his album and is given a few minutes to think about the content of the photos. The teacher can help with language.
5 The student describes his photos.
6 The teacher summarizes what the student has said.

Options

- A topic area can be targeted, for example:
  food – photos of a restaurant interior, dining room, celebration meal, family meal
  transport – photos of journeys, including train, aeroplane, car
  holidays – photos on the beach
  childhood – photos from childhood scenes
  family – family photos and gatherings
  sport – photos of sports events
- The summaries can be written or recorded on tape.
- The student can prepare questions to ask the teacher about her photos. The questions can be 'yes/no' questions only (*Is the photo black and white? Is it a holiday photo? Are you in the photo?* etc.).
- When working with a shy student, the teacher can ask him 'yes/no' questions about his photo.
- The student listens to the description of the teacher's photos and chooses his favourite photo to summarize.

A real photograph

The teacher brings in a photograph of a member of her family or a friend. The student makes predictions in the form of statements about the person in the photograph and the teacher indicates whether the statements are true or false. For example:

Student   (looking at a photograph of the teacher's teenage son) *He goes to school.*

Teacher	*True.*
Student	*He plays rugby at school.*
Teacher	*True.*
Student	*His favourite subject is English.*
Teacher	*False ...*

The student can then summarize all the information about the person photographed.

> **Sample Activity Sequence F**
>
> **Aim**: to practise spoken fluency talking about personal information.
>
> 1 The student makes statements about the person or persons in the photograph. The teacher indicates true or false.
> 2 The student summarizes orally all the information he can remember.
> 3 The teacher adds any missed information.

Options
- The student brings in a real photograph and the teacher makes guesses and deductions about the person. Finally, the teacher summarizes all of the true information. The teacher then dictates this to the student. The teacher checks for spelling and punctuation. The text can then be recorded on to tape by the teacher and then the student.
- To provide spoken accuracy as an aim, the teacher reformulates each of the student's statements before indicating if it is true or false.

Outside the window

Using the immediate environment outside the study room is a way of breaking out of the potentially confining work space. The student faces away from the window or the teacher closes the blinds or curtains and the student is asked to remember as much as he can – and in detail – of what can be seen. This provides practice in description and location language.

Sample Activity Sequence G

Aim: to practise description and location language.

1 The teacher closes the blinds or curtains or the student faces away from the window.
2 The student describes from memory everything that can be seen outside from the window.
3 The teacher summarizes orally what the student has said.
4 The curtains or blinds are opened or the student faces the window and the student is given a short time, say 15 seconds, to survey the view.
5 The student describes the view again from memory.
6 The teacher summarizes orally again.
7 The student is given another opportunity to check the view.
8 Student and then teacher produce final oral summaries.

Options

- Both teacher and student work individually to provide final written summaries. They read each other's to find differences between their versions. They can work on the student's script for language. The student can keep both versions. The two versions could be recorded on tape.
- The teacher draws up a list of questions about the view:
    How many traffic lights are there?
    What colour is the shop sign on the newsagent's?
  The student answers them before and after seeing the actual view. The student uses the list of questions as a prompt to summarize the view.
- The internal view outside the door of the study room is used.
- The inside of a room nearby is used in the same way.
- The teacher can present relevant vocabulary before doing the tasks.

The inner flashcard

The use of guided visualization provides a powerful way of importing people and places into the study space. The technique whereby the student closes his eyes and is asked to conjure up mental images with the teacher's guidance is used extensively in accelerative learning, drama, sports training and so on. The student sits comfortably and shuts his eyes. The teacher guides the visualization while the student summons up images internally and without speaking. This is a powerful activity in which the right side of the brain is engaged by the activity of visualization and then balanced with the left brain activity of describing the scene verbally.

It is probably a good idea to wait until you know the student quite well before doing guided visualization. Both student and teacher can feel awkward closing their eyes the first time you try the activity but it always seems to work! Close your eyes yourself in case the student takes a peek. This also makes it easier to attune yourself to the slower speed of delivery you need to adopt to give the student time to understand your instructions and then access images. Work through each of the senses in order to cater for different learner and representational styles. Include repetition and ensure that the language you use is well within the student's range. Unknown language may very well provoke a headache! It is important, too, not to introduce any negative elements into the visualization. Give the student plenty of time, a minute or so, to surface at the end. Some teachers put on background music, for example, slow Baroque pieces. Others feel that music is distracting and divides and weakens the attention. Guide and provide a framework for the student to create his own images rather than dictate what he should experience. So say, 'Notice the colour and size of the door' rather than, 'You see a large red front door' or 'Is the door big?'.

Sample Activity Sequence H

Aim: to practise describing the outside of a house.

In this example the teacher and student have been working on the language of describing houses.

1 The teacher asks the student to sit comfortably and close his eyes for a short time and to follow her instructions.
2 The teacher guides the student through the visualization.
You are standing in the street opposite a house ... See the colours and shapes of the house ... Notice how many windows and doors there are ... Feel the atmosphere and character of the house ... Hear sounds and noises in the street as you stand opposite the house ... Are there any smells around you in the street ...? Notice the weather as you stand opposite the house ... Look back at the house ... the colours, the shapes, the windows, the doors, the atmosphere and character ... Now take a minute to leave the house and return to the room ...

Take a minute to open your eyes slowly ...

3 The student summarizes orally what he experienced.
4 The teacher reformulates his description.
5 The student writes a description of the house visualized.

Options

• The student writes down the visualization immediately. Meanwhile the teacher writes down a description of a house, maybe her own. The student reads the teacher's description – the task is to find a given number of similarities and differences between his house and the teacher's.

• Clearly any scene can be imported into the room. Narrative and movement can be introduced within the visualization. Within his imagination the student can be invited to see and feel himself walk and perform actions and notice these.

> *You walk down the street ... Notice the people and cars around you ... You see a shop on your right ... What kind of shop is it ...? Go into the shop ... Notice what the assistant looks like ... You ask for something and pay for it ... Now leave the shop ...*

In a business context the student can visualize a successful interaction with a client. At the end there is the opportunity to re-tell the events and practise past tenses.

Phoning out

The use of the telephone provides one of the most real and authentic ways of peopling the study room. The teacher can give the student real practice in ringing out for information. This can include:

• ringing hotels and finding out about availability and cost of rooms, services and facilities provided
• finding out about travel information, times of trains, planes, fares
• phoning for entertainment information, availability and cost of tickets for theatre, concerts and sports events.

As part of the lesson preparation the teacher can make the phone call or calls in real time and make a note of what she says and in particular what is said by the person who answers the phone. With the right kind of answerphone facility the teacher can record both sides of her conversation or her own half of the conversation with a cassette recorder.

The teacher will now be able to prepare the student for the call. Both sides of the call could be transcribed or you could write out a version of the call and then cut up the lines for the student to put back into the right order. The teacher and student can then practise reading the parts aloud and with the option of recording the conversation. They can of course simply roleplay the call.

It is also useful to teach essential telephone language which tends to be very formulaic.

Useful language

* **Making/starting the call:**
  This is (Paul Heinrich).
  (Paul Heinrich) speaking.
  Is that (Maria Ruas)?
  Could I speak to (Maria Ruas)?
  Extension 123, please.

* **Problems:**
  I'll hold.
  I'll call back later.
  Could you take a message?
  Could you give (Maria) a message?
  Could you put me through to (her secretary)?
  It's a very bad line. Could I ring back?

* **Receiving the call:**
  (BBC). Can I help you?
  Speaking.
  Just a moment. I'll put you through.
  I'm afraid she's not in the office at the moment.
  I'm afraid she's in a meeting.
  I'm afraid the line's engaged.
  Would you like to hold?
  I'm putting you through.
  I'm sorry, I think you have the wrong number.
  Would you like to leave a message?

The telephone formulae can be input in different ways. They can be jumbled on cards for the student to reorder (*you hold would to like?*). The formulae can be written on slips or laminated card for the student to sort under headings, such as Start the call, Answer the call, Problems. To internalize the language the student scans the formulae, looks away or turns them over, and reproduces them orally and/or in writing. Use Cuisenaire rods to represent each word in the formulae and mark stress by placing rods on top of the appropriate words (see Unit 7, Cuisenaire Rods). The teacher can prompt the formulae by giving the student key words, such as *sorry, wrong, number*. Alternatively, gap the formulae (*I'm putting you _____*). After each correct reproduction of a formula, it can be recorded on tape by the student and also optionally by the teacher.

Sample Activity Sequence I

Aim: to practise telephone language and asking for hotel information.

1 The teacher gives the student a written jumbled telephone conversation about requesting hotel information. This will resemble in format and language the call he will make. The student arranges the lines of the dialogue in the correct order.
2 The teacher and student practise reading the correctly sequenced dialogue aloud. They take turns in reading each part.
3 The dialogue is recorded on tape with teacher and student taking turns to read each part.
4 The teacher and student roleplay the conversation without the script.
5 The student makes the phone call and reports back the information.

Options

- The teacher notes down errors the student makes while he is phoning. The teacher asks him to correct them after he has reported back on the call.
- With the appropriate answerphone facility, the teacher can record the conversation and replay it to clarify language used by the person on the other end of the line and to involve the student in correction of his own errors.
- The student can make another call or calls of a similar type to other organizations, such as another hotel or hotels.
- To replicate the telephone scenario the teacher can sit back to back with the student to roleplay the phone calls.

Postcards and props

With the use of pictures and props you can transform the study space into another environment. Measures such as these are extremely simple but produce a transformation of the learning environment which is surprisingly effective. For example, postcards or a place setting for a restaurant-based lesson bring the outside world into the classroom and add reality value.

Art gallery

The teacher can put some postcards or other reproductions of paintings around the study space on the walls or simply arranged around the desk top to create a gallery. Then the teacher takes the student into the 'gallery' and talks about the paintings.

Sample Activity Sequence J

Aim: to practise describing paintings.

1 The teacher focuses on some language relevant to talking about paintings (*abstract, portrait, landscape, still life, oil, watercolour*, etc).

2 The teacher shows the student around the gallery, talking about the paintings she likes. The teacher asks him what he likes and why.

3 The teacher gives the student a pack of postcards and asks him to select, say six, and to arrange an exhibition.

4 The student shows the teacher round.

Options

- The student can prepare his exhibition in advance of the lesson.
- In advance of the lesson the teacher records on tape a tour of her gallery. The task for the student is to put the postcards in the order in which she described them.
- In the absence of a tape recorder the teacher shows the student around the gallery and he puts the postcards in order as the teacher goes along.
- After the viewing of the gallery, the teacher spreads the postcards with the addition of a few extras on the table. The teacher describes one painting and the student has to wait until the teacher has finished before identifying which one she

described. Then the student describes a painting for the teacher to identify.

- The student can summarize the teacher's showing around the gallery and then the teacher summarizes the student's tour. This can be done orally and/or in writing as an exhibition review.
- As in the activity above with the virtual photo album, the teacher and later the student cuts out blank pieces of paper to represent the works of art. The teacher shows the student around the virtual gallery and vice versa.

Estate agent

Pictures of rooms either sketched or cut from magazines can be used to create a house or flat. The teacher shows the student around – he is a potential buyer. The student can also choose pictures of rooms to create a property and then show the teacher around.

Sample Activity Sequence K

Aim: to clarify, focus on and practise language relevant to asking and talking about property.

1 Present useful language, along the lines of the vocabulary of rooms and furniture and fittings. Include structures such as *There is/are ...*.

You can include local amenities: *five minutes' walk from the station*, *convenient for the shops*, etc.

2 The student prepares questions, say eight, to ask about the property.

3 The teacher works on the questions with him.

4 The teacher shows the student around and he asks questions.

5 The student summarizes everything he knows about the property.

6 Now the procedure is repeated with the student showing the teacher around his own property.

Options

- The property can be a flat or house to let. This can involve drawing up and asking questions about the house rules, especially if it's set up as a house-share with a group of tenants.
- The property can be virtual with blank pieces of paper or Cuisenaire rods (see Unit 7) to represent rooms.

Eating out

A restaurant scenario can be created with a few simple prompts – a menu (an authentic one from a local restaurant or restaurant chain or one manufactured by the teacher), a table cloth and place settings. The teacher can play the part of the waitress asking how many people are in the party and showing the student as client to the table and taking his order. Realistic and relevant practice can be provided with the student standing at the door of the study room and being welcomed by the teacher and shown to a table. Another stage of the role play can involve the teacher and student sitting at the table as though friends or in a business person–client situation. This can provide practice in choosing from the menu, making suggestions, and passing items at the table.

Sample Activity Sequence L

Aim: to clarify, focus on and practise language appropriate to visiting a restaurant.

1 The teacher discusses with the student the process involved in arriving at a restaurant and being shown to a table: announcing a reservation, if not, being asked how many people are in the party, whether smokers or non-smokers, and so on. The teacher goes over language appropriate at each step:
    I've reserved a table for two.
    In what name, please?
    How many is it for? Smokers or non-smokers?
2 The teacher and student roleplay the scenario.
3 The teacher elicits each line of the dialogue and writes it down prompting student self-correction when necessary.
4 The teacher and student practise reading the dialogue aloud and change roles.
5 The teacher and student record the dialogue on tape.

Options
• Other place-based scenarios can be treated in the same way:
    offering and passing food and drink at the table
    checking in at a hotel
    making travel enquiries at a station
    opening an account at a bank
    job interview in a company
    asking about clothes in a shop
    joining a library
    hiring a car in a car rental office
    sending letters and parcels at a post office.

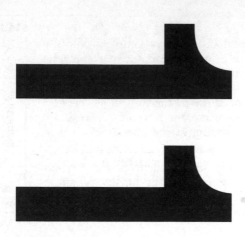

reading and listening

In this unit you will learn
- about developing your student's reading and listening skills
- how to personalize reading and listening tasks

Think about

The student is given an article to read about shopping in a supermarket. In which order would you ask the following questions:

a How does the article suggest saving money?
b What is the name of the supermarket?
c Is the article about shopping or sport?

The advantage of teaching only one student is clear when deciding on reading and listening materials and tasks, for these can be chosen and designed with the student's own interests and needs in mind. And, of course, the student can choose his own texts.

Materials

It is not necessary to use a coursebook and those without access to a photocopier need not worry. There is an endless variety of materials which can be used for **reading tasks**, including newspapers, magazines, timetables, leaflets, junk mail, flyers, CD or cassette notes, programmes, reference books (dictionaries, encyclopaedias, directories, recipe books), manuals, instructions, packaging (for ingredients, ways to use), fiction (novels and short stories in books or magazines).

For **listening tasks**, there are the radio (e.g. the BBC World Service), television, video, CDs, the telephone (the speaking clock, recorded information, ordering catalogues/brochures), sports commentary, tapes made by the teacher.

Tasks

It is hard to imagine focusing one's attention on reading or listening to something for no reason. It is important that the student has a reason to read or listen in his English lessons, just as he would in his native language. The teacher's saying, *Please read this* is not helpful and may be off-putting. Rather than concentrating on the text, the student spends the time wondering what on earth the teacher has in store when he has finished it. Does the teacher think he will be capable of understanding it? What if he doesn't understand it? What if the teacher asks him a question and he can't remember the answer? Will he be allowed to look at or listen to the piece again? The nervous student might be genuinely concerned about looking foolish.

Recordings or pages of print can be extremely daunting. The teacher can show the student that, however apparently 'difficult' the piece, he can get something out of it. The elementary student can identify numbers or nationalities from an article in the *Financial Times*.

There are different ways to approach a text or recording. To use a swimming pool analogy: one can dive straight in or test the water first, starting at the shallow end and progressing towards the deep end. The option generally considered to be the most student-friendly is to provide a non-threatening opportunity for the student to gain an impression of the text or recording before expecting him to read it for detail. It may be that detailed reading is not required at all. Whatever the role (whether reading as himself or 'in character') adopted by the student, no matter what the material used, this procedure can be followed:

Standard Reading Format	Standard Listening Format
Lead-in	Lead-in
Prediction	Prediction
and/or	and/or
*Skimming	*Gist listening/tuning-in
and/or	and/or
*Scanning	*Listening to extract information
Intensive reading	Intensive listening

*These tasks will work more effectively if the teacher explains to the student that he does not need to understand everything. In the case of skim or scan reading, giving the student a brief time limit will encourage him not to read every word.

Lead-in

This sets the scene, triggers memories, gives the student time to recall relevant vocabulary and generally avoid going in cold to a text or tape. New vocabulary, key to the understanding of the materials, could be clarified here.

Prediction

The student could be asked to predict the likely content of the piece by looking at the headline, title or accompanying picture. He then reads or listens in order to check the prediction. It is unimportant whether or not he predicts correctly; the point of the task is partly to generate interest in the topic and partly to give a reason for reading or listening.

Tuning-in

The task might be as simple as identifying the number, sex, approximate age or mood of the speaker(s). The student who has real difficulty with listening comprehension will benefit from this gentle way in. Research suggests that a native speaker listening to an unfamiliar presenter on the radio will need several seconds to tune in to the new voice.

Skimming

Skim reading or 'skim listening' can be for the gist of the piece, i.e.

its subject matter (families, coal mining, the future)
its tone (friendly, serious, rude)
its degree of formality (formal, neutral, informal)
its purpose (to advertise, to invite, to warn)
its likely origin (newspaper, scientific paper, recipe, weather forecast)

Scanning/listening to extract information

A text or recording containing several names (as long as the student is familiar with these, otherwise they may pass unnoticed), numbers or dates lends itself to these sub-skills, because these are things which tend to stand out from the rest of the piece.

While the student is focusing on one of these sub-skills, he will not need to worry about the details or all the words he does not understand.

Intensive reading/listening

After completing achievable, confidence-building tasks, such as skimming and scanning, the student is better prepared to undertake tasks involving detailed reading or listening.

The most obvious benefit of teaching one student only is that he can read or listen to what interests him. This may or may not require preparation by the teacher. The following sequence of activities requires none. It provides the student with reading comprehension practice and, as it is he who decides what to read, it is perhaps a more motivating task than one set by the teacher.

Reading

Dense text can be daunting, yet the student may be keen to read the article, knowing its subject matter is of interest to him. By deciding what he wants to find out before reading, the student provides a way in. In the following activity, the student is looking for answers to his own questions. It is possible that the article may not contain these. This is something which reflects 'real life' experiences. If the student is particularly keen to find the answers, there is the option of looking in other newspapers, watching the news, or surfing the Internet etc.

Sample Activity Sequence A

Aim: to practise skimming and intensive reading skills.

1 The student is given a newspaper and asked to skim through it in order to find two or three articles which he thinks he would find interesting. The student makes his decision based on the headline and/or photograph.
2 Having done this, the student skims the articles and chooses the one which appeals the most.
3 The teacher encourages the student to talk about what he already knows about the story or the subject in general.
4 The student decides what he would like to find out and writes a series of questions to which he expects to find the answers in the article.
5 The student reads the text to find the answers to his questions. He writes these down.
6 The student reports back to the teacher, using his notes, not reading from the text.
7 The student writes or gives an oral summary of the article.

Options

- Rather than writing the answers, the student simply tells the teacher what he finds out.
- The student skims the paper for one article only and predicts its content from the headline or photograph before writing the questions.
- The student writes a number of statements predicting the content of the article. He then reads the article to find out whether they are true or false.
- If the student has problems finding the answers to his questions, either because they are not there or because of his lack of language, the teacher can ask him some questions. If the teacher can see the text, she can scan it for suitable questions. If not, the teacher will have to think up questions relating to matters which are bound to be in the article, the most obvious being names, ages and dates.
- If the student is having difficulty understanding the article because of the vocabulary, this of course provides an opportunity to focus on it.
- Rather than presenting a student with a newspaper, which some might find daunting, the teacher chooses three articles and asks the student to skim them all and to choose the one he finds the most interesting. By setting a time limit and a specific task, such as *What is the topic of each story?* the teacher discourages the student from intensive reading.
- Students at advanced levels predict the likely tone (e.g. sarcastic, ironic) of a piece, the clues to this being in the headline.

If the story is an ongoing one, the student and teacher follow its progress. The teacher must be sure, however, that the student wishes to do so and should stop if he loses interest. The story may, of course, be followed in newspapers – perhaps comparing the reporting of it in a selection of papers – or on the radio or television news. The student could write a review of the story so far, adding to it as new developments arise.

Listening

The teacher may have a particular reason for restricting the number of times the student listens to the recording (perhaps he is going to go to university and needs practice in note taking at lectures, where there will only be one opportunity to listen).

Otherwise, it is helpful if the student knows that he can listen to the recording as many times as necessary. After all, the tasks are designed to help him practise listening skills. To avoid appearing to be testing the student's memory, the teacher needs to set the tasks before playing the tape.

Sample Activity Sequence B

Aim: to practise listening for gist and intensive listening.

1 The teacher pre-records a television or radio news programme.
2 The student and teacher discuss topical news stories. The student predicts which will be on the news.
3 The student listens to or watches the news headlines, with the task of checking his predictions. He need only listen for gist at this stage.
4 Answers are confirmed and the student chooses one story on which to focus.
5 The student writes a number of questions to which he expects to find the answers in the part of the programme which deals with the chosen news story.
6 The student listens to or watches the relevant report and writes the answers as he hears them.
7 The student listens or watches again to confirm the answers. He has control of the machine, so that he can replay all or part of the report as often as necessary (just as he would have the opportunity to re-read a text).
8 He reports back to the teacher.

Options

• At lower levels, the student can count the number of headlines. He may be able to do this by listening to the change in pitch of the newsreader's voice alone. He could then be asked to identify the topic of each headline. Other ideas include making a note of the numbers or place names he hears in a particular story.
• Having predicted the stories which might appear in the bulletin and in which order, the student watches to confirm his prediction of that order.

The same student-centred approach can be adopted for other publications and programmes. The point is that the student provides the task – the reason for reading, whether it is skimming a cookery book to find a suitable recipe for a certain occasion (and perhaps then cooking it, which would require intensive reading skills) or listening to the weather forecast the day before a planned trip.

Roles

The material itself may suggest a task, which in turn suggests a role. Take, for example, a holiday brochure. The student's task is to choose a holiday destination and accommodation within a certain budget and time period. The student is given the role of family breadwinner.

See the table on page 159 for some ideas for combining materials, roles and tasks.

> ## Sample Activity Sequence C
>
> **Aim**: to practise scanning and intensive reading skills.
>
> 1 As a lead-in, the teacher and student talk about favourite holidays they have had, dream holidays or something similar.
> 2 The teacher provides a photograph of a family or other group of people, together with a budget, and asks the student to take on the role of one of the family members. The student first decides on the criteria (location, accommodation, leisure acitivities, etc.) and then begins the search.
> 3 Using a number of holiday brochures, the student scans the pages for a holiday which appears to fulfil the criteria.
> 4 He then reads relevant parts more intensively in order to choose a destination.
> 5 The student repeats the exercise, taking on the role of a different member of the group.

Options

- Following the activity, the student compares the two types of holiday chosen by different members of the family. This could be done orally or in writing.
- The teacher provides the criteria for the holiday as well as the people and budget.
- The teacher prepares for the lesson by cutting out details of a number of different holidays from which the student chooses.
- The teacher prepares for the lesson by cutting out details of a number of different holidays and providing details of a number of family groups. The student matches families to holidays, explaining how he has made the selection.

Of course, television and video are invaluable sources of listening materials, with the added benefit of pictures (though the picture can be turned off if required). The teacher who knows a student's interests can be on the look-out for any likely interviews, such as with politicians on news programmes. These are generally fairly short.

Some argue that there is no need to provide students with a skimming, scanning or equivalent task, as long as the text or recording is of sufficient interest. Sample Activity Sequence D goes straight to intensive listening without any tuning-in, gist listening or listening for specific information task.

Sample Activity Sequence D

Aim: to practise intensive listening.

1 The student is told that he is going to watch a short television interview with, in this case, a politician who has been in the news recently and with whose story the student is familiar. The student recalls what he knows.
2 The student puts himself in the role of interviewer and prepares a list of questions which he thinks will be asked.
3 The student listens to the interview, ticking off the questions if he hears them. (This requires more than listening for gist; exact wording may be crucial.)
4 The student listens again, this time for answers to the questions he has written.
5 If able to, the student discusses the answers with the teacher. However, if his questions are not answered in the interview, he listens again to make a note of the questions which are asked.
6 The student listens again to find out the answers.

Options

- The student writes down the questions he anticipates being asked and listens first for these. Having ascertained which of these have been asked, he then listens for answers. If none has been asked, the student could be asked to take notes and then summarize what the politician has been saying.
- The student is given the questions asked (on laminated strips) and puts them in the order in which they are asked as he listens. He then listens again for the answers.
- The student is given the questions asked and predicts the politician's answers. He then listens to confirm the predictions.

The tape can be played as many times as the student needs to confirm his understanding. The more sure the student is of what he is listening to, the sooner confidence will grow.

	Materials	Role	Task
R	newspaper: job ads	self/student	find a job
R	catalogue	grandparent on a budget	Christmas presents for grandchildren
R L	ringroad development proposal	eco-warrior/local resident	find two angles in same story
R	week's television schedule	pop music fan	find programmes fan would like
R L	information about museums	tourist with particular interest	choose a museum
R	entertainment guide	student	plan a weekend's fun
R L	film review	self (no role)	decide whether or not to see it
L	radio phone-in	agony aunt/uncle	give advice
L	cookery programme	self	take down recipe
L	advertisement for fast food	child/parent	arguments for/against eating it
L	interview	interviewer	write questions beforehand and listen for answers

R = Reading task   L = Listening task

12

storyboard – text restoration

In this unit you will learn
- how to use the technique of 'total cloze' to prompt language use by your student

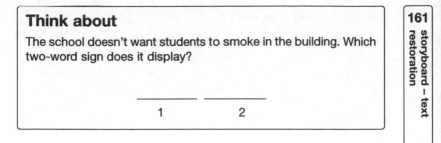

Think about

The school doesn't want students to smoke in the building. Which two-word sign does it display?

_____ _____

1   2

Storyboard

There is a vast array of programs available for English language training. *Storyboard* is a commercially produced authoring program which is very useful when working one to one. Storyboard allows the teacher to type in any text. The computer program deletes the text, replacing each word with a series of asterisks and leaving only the punctuation. The task for the student is to restore the text by typing in any words he thinks may appear in it. The computer inserts correct words in all of the places in which they appear until the text has been restored in its entirety. To give a very simple example, if the teacher is working on signs which appear in public places, she may type in among others:

   No smoking.

The computer deletes the text as follows:

   ** *******.

If the student types in 'smoking', the computer restores the word:

   ** *smoking.*

Of course, the student can offer the word and the teacher can type it in to ensure correct spelling. Otherwise it is important for the teacher to monitor the student's spelling as he is typing to avoid frustration on the student's part.

The technique itself can still be used in the absence of a computer, as explained later in this unit.

Student generated text

The technique whereby the teacher reformulates a piece of student writing can be used to good advantage with the aid of Storyboard (see Unit 5, Reformulation).

Sample Activity Sequence A

Aim: to reformulate a spoken description with accuracy.

1 The teacher asks the student to tell her briefly about where he lives – in about six sentences. She listens without intervention.
2 The student repeats his description slowly and the teacher types the text, reformulated correctly into the Storyboard authoring program. The student doesn't see the text being typed.
3 The text is deleted using the program.
4 The student restores his own reformulated description by typing in words he thinks are there. The computer inserts them or rejects them if not in the text or if misspelled. The teacher prompts the student if necessary.
5 Once the text is restored, the student tells the teacher again orally about where he lives.
6 The teacher prints off the text for the student's record.
7 The teacher records the text on to tape.
8 The student reads out and records the text on to tape.

Options

- The student watches as the teacher types in the reformulation of his spoken text. In this way he witnesses the juxtaposition of his own language with the reformulation.
- The student provides the teacher with a written description of where he lives. The teacher types a reformulation into the Storyboard program for the student to restore. The written reformulation could be done by the teacher between sessions and the text restoration completed by the student as a review.
- Dialogue or role play between the teacher and student can be used in a similar way. After the oral work, student and teacher collaborate to type in the script. Where the interchange is lengthy, then just a part of the conversation can be written up.

Teacher generated text

This section looks at ways in which the student can be prompted and guided to restore texts the teacher has already prepared.

Prediction

The student is given information about the topic of a text and he predicts words that may come up. These are typed in and inserted by the program if correct. For example:

This text is about crime in London.

The student is asked to offer nouns and verbs such as *burglary, increased,* etc.

Where the text is a dialogue, the teacher can give the function and the setting or situation. For example:

> *Mr Jenkins makes a complaint to the waiter about the soup in an Italian restaurant.*

Pre-set questions

Provide a set of questions on the text:

> *Where did John go on Thursday?*

From this question the student will probably type in *John, Thursday, went.* After the text has been largely or partly restored, the student answers the questions.

'Yes/no/not important' questions

The teacher gives some key words from the text, such as *umbrella, nightmare, Calcutta.* The student asks 'yes/no' questions and the teacher replies: *yes, no,* or *not important.* For example:

> *Did someone lose an umbrella in Calcutta?*
> *Yes.*

As information is uncovered, the student offers words to the program, such as *lost.* As the text is revealed, more questions can be asked until the text is fully restored. Finally, the student can retell the story or summarize the text orally before being given a print-out.

Delayed dictation

The teacher reads out or orally retells/summarizes a text. When the summary is finished, the student works on text restoration.

Information transfer

The student is given a text, for example, a completed application form, and this acts as a prompt for the restoration of a text containing the same information. For example:

Surname: *Morello*	First Name: *Rosa*
Nationality: *Colombian*	Occupation: *Student*
Age: *18*	Interests: *English, dance*

The on-screen text for restoration would be as follows:

> * .
> * * * * * * * * * * * * * . *
> * * * * * * * . * * * * * * 18 * * * * * * * * . * * * * * * * * * * * * * *
> * * * * * * * * * .
>
> Rosa Morello is from Colombia in South America. She is a student. She has come to London to study English. Rosa is 18 years old. She likes English and dancing.

Alternatively, the student could be given the paragraph and asked to restore the form on screen. Clearly, a lot of material will lend itself to information transfer of this kind. For example:

Prompt text	On screen text
• graph of sales	• account of sales in prose
• family tree	• prose description of family
• map with directions	• written directions

Summaries

The student restores a text which summarizes a reading passage or listening material already worked on. Where the summary is of a conversation, features of reporting speech can be highlighted and practised. For example, on tape:

Jane   *Let's go out for a pizza.*
Max   *OK, good idea.*

Text to restore:

> * . * * *
> * .
>
> Jane suggested going out for a pizza. Max thought it was a good idea.

Visual input

The student is given a picture and the text to restore is a description of that picture. The student is given a picture story and the teacher elicits a narrative in the past tense. The teacher has already typed in a version of the storyline or the teacher types in a correct version of the storyline as the student offers it. The student's task is to restore the storyline.

Transformations

The student is given instructions in the *active voice*, the text to restore is in the *passive voice*. Exercises in the style of public examinations can also be carried out this way. For example, the student is given the sentence:

Can I use your phone?

The student is then asked to type in another way of making the request, in this case a more formal way.

Text to restore:

> * ****** ** * ***** *** **** *****.
> I wonder if I could use your phone.

Situational prompts

The on screen text is prompted with a mini-situation. For example:

You are leaving a party. What do you say to the host/hostess?

Text to restore:

> * **** ** ** ***** ***. ***** *** *** * ******
> **** *******.
> I have to be going now. Thank you for a really nice evening.

No computer?

The Storyboard technique of text deletion can be used without a computer. For example, the student describes where he lives in six sentences. The student repeats the task, providing the description for the teacher to reformulate in writing. The teacher numbers each sentence and each word after reformulation. The teacher takes a separate sheet of paper and produces a gapped version of the reformulation with the same numbering system. For example, here are the first two reformulated sentences:

Student's original words:

I live Peru. Me house is in city centre.

Reformulated text:

```
I  live  in  Peru.
1   2    3    4
My house is in the city centre.
 1      2   3 4 5   6     7
```

Deleted version:

```
___  ___  ___  ___  .
 1    2    3    4

___  ___  ___  ___  ___  ___  ___  .
 1    2    3    4    5    6    7
```

The student suggests a word and if correct the teacher writes it in. This continues until the text is restored.

Something to talk about cards

Here are some topic ideas for 'Something to talk about' cards (see Unit 1, The First Lesson).

My family	*My best friend*
My ambitions	*A happy memory*
My job	*My country*

resources and ideas bank

My home

A person I admire

Something I'm proud of

A memorable journey

My pet

A favourite artist

A special place

My favourite kind of music

Something I feel strongly about

what makes me laugh

Other topic suggestions

My best/worst/cheapest/most expensive/most exciting holiday.
My best/worst/most interesting/most boring/most stressful job.
The oldest/youngest/most interesting/most admirable/friendliest person I know.
The most beautiful/dirtiest/most peaceful/busiest/noisiest/farthest (from home) place I have visited.
My hobbies and interests.
Something I would never do again.
My ideal home/day/job/partner/holiday.
My first memory.
The best thing/worst thing/most surprising thing/thing that makes me most proud of my country.
My colleagues/business associates.
The hierarchy of my company/school/organization.
My best learning experiences.
An accident I had.
My worst illness.
My plans for next year/my studies/my career/my life.
An amazing dream I had.
The person I like most.
The three most important people in my life.
The three most important objects/places to me.
Three famous people (from history) I would like to meet and why.
The most important book/film/play/poem/song/sculpture/painting to me.
Ways I have changed.
Ways my job/family/country/the world has changed.
Three things I would like to change in my life.
How I feel about growing old.
The last five items I bought.
The last time I got angry/I was really happy.

Original tapescript

It is very easy to make a recording to use with students. The above topics could be used. These three questions were put to four native English speakers:

How old is the oldest person you know?
When does old age begin?
How do you feel about getting old?

Their spontaneous responses were recorded. Following the tapescript are some ideas for tasks.

Speaker 1 (male voice)

Um ... well, the oldest person I know, er ... that's close to me – is my mother. And she's nearly 80 now. I think old age really begins when you can't do what you used to do when you were younger. Um ... but it's ... a lot of it's in the mind, really. I don't mind getting old if I'm still healthy, if I can still travel and do lots of different things and play sports, but I don't want to get old if I'm going to be ill and unhealthy and sick.

Speaker 2 (female voice)

The oldest person I know is actually my mother, because, um ... she's 66 and my grandparents would be in their hundreds by now if they hadn't died, so I don't actually know anyone who's older than my mother. Um ... and we get on quite well, but because she's that much older than me – I'm 27 – she tends to not understand my life, sometimes, and she thinks I'm a bit crazy! Um ... I think old age ... ooh ... I think old age begins when you begin to *feel* old, 'cause I know that I'm not *really* old, I'm – as I said – I'm 27. But, when I go to bars and clubs, I see people that look younger than me, which makes me actually worry! And sometimes, when I look in the mirror, I see wrinkles, so, like does that mean I'm getting old? I don't know. I'm *horrified* at the thought of getting old. I really, really don't want to be old. I want to be like one of those ladies like, um ... Raquel Welch or Zsa Zsa Gabor or um ... I don't know. Anyone that's sort of has ... er ... kept their looks for a long time. But I don't think I'm actually doing that well already, so I doubt if I will be one of those!

Speaker 3 (male voice)

Er ... the oldest person I know, um ... is my mum, who was ... er ... let me think ... She was born in 1916 so she's now ... 85. Old age, when does it begin? Um ... that's a very interesting question, isn't it? Um ... it probably depends on the person. Old age probably begins at 20 for some people and ... er ... never begins at all for other people. Um ... yeah, I'm OK. It's quite exciting. Er ... I'd like to live for a lot, lot, lot, lot, lot, lot longer than I have, so I'm looking forward to seeing how everything changes around me. So I'm OK with that.

Speaker 4 (male voice)

My great uncle, Carmine, is 89 years old. He lives in Naples. I think old age begins when you feel it begins, but, um ... I guess the general idea is that old age is ... 60. How I feel about getting old ... is that I don't really want to get really old. I'd rather die first. Um ... I feel that when I'm really old and not capable of doing things that I would like to do, there is no point living.

Suggestions for using the recording

These are examples of tasks which could be given to the student. It is not intended for all these tasks to be set. The teacher might choosing a tuning-in task, followed by a gist listening task and then an intensive listening task. Alternatively, the teacher might select a prediction task only (it is necessary to set tasks whose answers will not overlap). The important thing to remember is to *set the task before playing the recording*. This reassures the student. (See Unit 11, Reading and Listening.)

Options: lead-in

- The teacher asks the student for his own answers to the three questions above.
- The teacher and student brainstorm vocabulary under the heading 'Old Age'. (This could form the basis of a listening task: the student listens for these words on the tape.) At this stage, the teacher can feed in any appropriate lexis.
- The student looks at photographs of elderly people and guesses their ages, hypothesises about their lives.
- The student is given photographs of people of various ages and considers the differences and similarities between their lives.

Options: tuning-in tasks

- How many people are speaking?
- How many men and how many women are speaking?
- How old do you think they are?

Options: prediction tasks

- The student has the three questions and the ages of the speakers. The teacher asks:
  What do you think their answers will be?
  Having predicted answers, the student listens to find out if he is right – entailing gist, e.g. the speaker seems to be optimistic, as the student predicted, or intensive listening skills, e.g. the student can give more detail.
- The student has the three questions. The teacher asks him to list ten words he thinks he will hear. As the student listens to the recording, he ticks off those words he hears – entailing listening to extract specific information.
- The teacher gives the student a list of about ten words, perhaps including some which are not on the tape. The student ticks those words he thinks he will hear and then listens to check the predictions, ticking off those words he hears and comparing the two lots of ticks – listening to extract specific information.

Options: listening to extract specific information

- (See prediction tasks, above.)
- How old is the oldest person each speaker knows?
- Write down all the numbers you hear.

Options: listening for gist

- Which speaker feels the most negative about getting old, and which the most positive?
- Match the gist to the speaker:

    Speaker _____ wants to live for a very long time.

    Speaker _____ seems most concerned about physical appearance.

    Speaker _____ thinks it's better to die than be very old.

    Speaker _____ thinks it's all right to be old if you can continue to do what you enjoy.

- What are the three questions that each speaker has been asked?

Options: intensive listening

- Whose view is closest to your own?
- Make notes as you are listening and afterwards write a one-sentence summary of what each speaker says.
- Answer the following questions:

    Speaker 1 – What are his interests?

    Speaker 2 – What is she most worried about?

    Speaker 3 – Why does he want to live for a long time?

    Speaker 4 – Why would he prefer to die than be really old?

Options: follow-up tasks

- The student writes or records his answers to the same questions. These could then be reformulated as described in Unit 5.

- The recording is used as a resource for language work. From the above tapescript, the teacher might choose to focus on comparative adjectives, such as *older, younger, longer than*. After a tuning-in or similar task, the student is given the tapescript with the comparatives blanked out. As the student listens again, he fills the gaps. This done, there is clarification of the structure and function. Other ideas include focusing on ways of talking about the future:

    I don't mind getting old if I can still travel.

    I don't want to get old if I'm going to be ill.

    I doubt I will be one of those ...

    When I'm really old ...

– and deducing the meaning of words and phrases from the
context, such *as a lot of; it's in the mind; horrified; kept their
looks; there is no point living.*

Exploiting a text

Not having access to published reading materials is no barrier to
practising reading skills. The teacher can very easily prepare her
own. This text is an original interview conducted by the author
and then written up. Suggestions for tasks follow.

GLOBETROTTER
An Interview with a Traveller

I – Interviewer   **C** – Catherine

I   What was the first country you ever visited?
C   Ever visited? France. I was so young I can't remember which
    part of France.
I   Do you remember much about the holiday?
C   No, I don't.
I   Which other countries have you been to?
C   Well, I've been to Spain, the USA, Australia, New Zealand,
    India, Nepal, Peru, Bolivia, Germany, Tanzania, Kenya,
    Indonesia, Malaysia, Holland a few times, Greece, Scotland,
    Ireland, Wales, the Czech Republic. I've passed through
    Austria. Oh – Egypt. Canada – only to cross the border.
    Oh, and Argentina and Uruguay, but they were only to cross the
    border to see the waterfalls on the other side. Oh, and a bit of
    Mexico.
I   How do you usually travel?
C   Aeroplanes and buses. When I'm in the country, I usually travel
    by bus. Occasionally, I've hired a car or I've shared cars with
    other travellers. Or the train. Mostly cars.
I   Are there any places or things that stand out?
C   Yes. I think seeing Uluru* – considering it was just a big rock in
    the middle of nowhere – it was pretty awesome. And I also
    thought the Taj Mahal was very mysterious, because I saw it in
    the early morning and as the mist rose it just appeared –
    magical, mysterious, very romantic.
I   Have you ever eaten anything that you wouldn't normally eat?
C   I'm afraid … yes. I've eaten guinea pig, which was pretty sad.
I   Why did you eat it?
C   Because that's all we were given when we were staying in
    somebody's home and all we had to eat was what they gave us

and that included three sweet potatoes each and a joint of
guinea pig.

I What do you like best about travelling?

C What do I like best? Seeing the wonders of the world and
meeting the people.

I What do you like least?

C Arriving at a train station at 3.00 in the morning, not knowing
where to go. I wouldn't do that any more.

I Have you stayed in touch with any of the people you've met on
your trips?

C Yes, I have. Yes. And they are the people I'm closest to now.

I Where would you like to go next?

C Um … Somewhere new. I'd like to go to Alaska, but I probably
won't go there next, because it's far away and expensive to get
around and you'd have to camp.

I Thank you for talking to me about your travel experiences.

C It was a pleasure.

*Also known as Ayers Rock

Options: lead-in

- The student lists as many countries as he can, either orally or
in writing or both. Or he lists countries he has visited and
ones he would like to visit and why.

- The student talks about his own travel experiences.

- The teacher feeds some of the vocabulary into the lead-in (for
example, *border, waterfall, awesome, mist, mysterious,
guinea pig*).

Options: prediction tasks

- The student is asked what he thinks 'globetrotter' means and
therefore what the interview might be about.

- The student writes some questions he would ask Catherine
and then scans the text to see if the same questions appear.

- The student is shown photographs of famous landmarks of
the countries mentioned and names the countries. He
confirms his answers by scanning the interview for these.

- The student is given oral clues about some of the countries
mentioned, for example, *Which country has kangaroos?* and
writes down which country he thinks it is. He then scans the
interview to confirm his answers.

Options: scanning tasks

- See prediction tasks above.

- The student writes down the names of as many countries as
he can in thirty seconds and then scans the text to see how
many of these appear.

- The teacher gives the student a list of words and he ticks those which he imagines will appear in the interview. He then scans it to see if he is right.

Options: skimming tasks

- The teacher gives the student two summaries of the interview. The student skims the interview in order to choose the best summary. (Example: *Catherine talks about her experiences of travelling around the world* or *Catherine talks about her favourite countries*).
- The student is given a choice of titles and skims the text in order to choose the best one. (Example: *Catherine's Travels*; *A Terrible Meal*; *Waterfalls*). He justifies his choice.

Options: intensive reading

- The student comments on the following statements, referring to the text but expressing himself in his own words where possible:

   Catherine has been to Holland more times than she has been anywhere else.

   She is not surprised that she was so impressed by Uluru.

   She ate guinea pig meat unwillingly.

   She would probably feel more comfortable if she knew where she was going to stay on arrival at a new place.

   She has remained friendly with some of her travelling companions.

   Catherine doesn't think she will ever go to Alaska.

- The student answers the following questions orally or in writing:

   Why doesn't Catherine remember much about her first holiday abroad?

   Why did she go to Argentina?

   What reason does she give for eating guinea pig meat?

   Why didn't she like arriving at stations at 3.00 a.m.?

   What kind of accommodation does she expect she would stay in in Alaska?

- The student is encouraged to read between the lines and speculate in order to respond to the following questions:

   Why do you think Catherine was reluctant to eat guinea pig meat?

   Why do you think she says about arriving at a station at 3.00 a.m., not knowing where to go, 'I wouldn't do that any more'?

   Why do you think she is so close to her former travelling companions?

Options: follow up tasks

- The student considers the question, *Is there a difference between a tourist and a traveller?* either orally, in discussion with the teacher, or in writing.

- The student responds to the questions from the interview himself, either orally or in writing. This could then be reformulated. (See Unit 5, Reformulation.) The interview could also be conducted using the 'empty chair' technique. (See Unit 10, Peopling and Placing the Room.)

- Language work might focus on the use of the present perfect to talk about experience. The student underlines all the examples of *have* + past participle that he can find and the teacher asks him questions in order to guide him towards understanding its function, for example, *I've been to Spain. Do we know when?* Alternatively, the use of gerunds (e.g. <u>seeing</u> *the wonders of the world;* <u>arriving</u> *at a train station;* <u>not knowing</u> *where to go*) could be the focus. There are also a number of phrases to do with location (e.g. *to pass through, to cross the border, the other side, in the middle of nowhere*), which could be highlighted. Another idea is to focus on the pronunciation and word stress of countries and nationalities, adding to Catherine's list with places relevant to the student.

Consequences

This 'after dinner' game is fun and the simplest kind of story writing. When read aloud, it works well if the past simple tense is used.

Each person has a narrow piece of paper. The idea is that each writes names, places and speech, swapping the pieces of paper each time, so that the end result is a strange, usually nonsensical story written by two authors who don't know what the other has written. It is important that the names chosen are known to both players, either personally or because they are famous. This game works even better with more people!

How to play – instructions from the teacher to student

At the top of the paper, write the name of a famous man or a man we both know. Fold the paper over so that I can't see the name.

Swap pieces of paper.

Below the fold in the piece of paper – and on the same side – write the name of a famous woman or a woman we both know. Fold the paper over as before.

Swap pieces of paper.

Write a place where the man and woman met. (It could be anywhere: under a tree, in front of Buckingham Palace, in the cupboard under the stairs, at the top of a pyramid and so on.) Fold the paper over.

Swap pieces of paper.

Write what the man said to the woman. Fold the paper over.

Swap pieces of paper.

Write what the woman said to the man. Fold the paper over.

Swap pieces of paper.

Write the consequence. What happened at the end of the story? (For example, they kissed and said good-bye forever, they went to tea at The Ritz, they never spoke to each other again, they went to watch cricket at Lord's). Fold the paper over.

Swap pieces of paper and read the story aloud.

This is read aloud as:

Michael Jackson met Cleopatra on top of the Eiffel Tower. He said, 'Can you play table tennis?'. She said, 'I've never been to Guatemala.' The consequence was (or 'in the end') they swam from Italy to Greece and danced under an olive tree in the moonlight.

Phonemic symbols and some words in which they appear

/ɑː/	arm	/b/	bed
/æ/	apple	/d/	do
/aɪ/	eye	/f/	fill
/aʊ/	out	/g/	good
/e/	pen	/h/	hat
/eɪ/	eight	/j/	yes
/eə/	wear	/k/	kick
/ɪ/	sit	/l/	lose
/iː/	seat	/m/	me
/ɪə/	near	/n/	no
/ɒ/	on	/p/	put
/əʊ/	open	/r/	run
/ɔː/	always	/s/	soon
/ɔɪ/	boy	/t/	talk
/ʊ/	wood	/v/	very
/uː/	you	/w/	win
/ʊə/	tourist	/z/	zoo
/ɜː/	bird	/ʃ/	ship
/ʌ/	up	/ʒ/	measure
/ə/	doctor	/ŋ/	sing
		/tʃ/	cheap
		/θ/	theatre
		/ð/	then
		/dʒ/	June

Useful websites

The following websites are sources of materials, lesson ideas and homework.

http://www.guardian.co.uk
This site maintains an archive of articles from previous editions. Type in a search for the topic you want to cover with your student and you will be given a list of articles. This allows for the provision of instant reading material.

http://www.telegraph.co.uk
Similar to the *Guardian* website.

http://www.gvenglish.com
A feature of this expanding website is a teacher-led chat room and regular teacher-led online lessons. Topics for the lessons are posted in advance.

http://www.britishcouncil.org
This site contains teaching ideas and materials.

http://www.englishpage.com
This contains lessons and language exercises and includes online dictionaries and a thesaurus.

http://www.edufind.com
This site includes a diagnostic test to indicate the student's level and features a grammar clinic.

http://www.angelfire.com/az2/webenglish
This site has ideas for homework, including webquests.

glossary

This is a list of some of the terms that you will encounter in the profession – most of these terms have featured in the units.

abstract nouns   These refer to qualities and ideas rather than concrete items. So, *love, courage, unemployment, law and order* are abstract (*chair, energy* are concrete).

affixation   This is when prefixes (e.g. *dis-, un-, il-*) or suffixes (e.g. *-less, -ful, -able*) are put at the beginning or end of a word (e.g. *dissatisfied, careless*).

articles   *the* (definite article), *an, a* (indefinite article), and zero (i.e. when there is none).
   Love is all you need.

auditory learners   Learners who learn through listening; they access, recall and represent information to themselves in sounds.

auxiliary   An auxiliary verb which is used in conjunction with the infinitive or participle of another verb in order to form:
   negatives – *Sara **doesn't** drink.*
   questions – ***Do** they speak English?*
   tenses – *David **has been** playing cricket.*
or for emphasis – *I **do** live here!*
See also **modals**.

catenation   This is the term used to describe the liaison of the final consonant sound of one word with the first vowel sound of the next:
   get‿into, look‿away

clarify and focus   The process of analysing language: its form and meaning.

cline   This is a graded sequence or scale of degree:

amusing, funny, hilarious
minute, tiny, small, large, huge, vast

collocation   These are words which tend to go together for no easily definable reason:
have a cup of tea
barely audible
spring to the rescue
ulterior motive

comparative adjectives   Adjectives which are used to compare. Regular comparatives are formed by adding *-er* to the adjective.
older *than me*
bigger *than a mouse*
Longer adjectives are made into comparatives by the addition of *more*:
more realistic *than this picture*
There are also irregular comparatives such as **worse** from *bad*, **farther** from *far*.

concrete nouns   These are names of things available to the five senses. So *a painting, a stool, fish, perfume* are concrete nouns. (See **abstract nouns**.)

context   When presenting a language item, the teacher can put it into a verbal or visual context, perhaps in order to elicit the language from the student. For example, the teacher says:
'You are going to see Michael Jackson. You have a ticket for his concert on Saturday. But on Saturday, he is ill. He can't sing or dance! There is no concert on Saturday. But – no problem. He'll do another concert next Tuesday. So, you can see Michael Jackson on Tuesday. The date of the concert is different. It's later, because there was a problem. What's the word we need if we want to say that the date of something has changed? The concert is …'
If the student knows it, he gives the word; if not, the teacher tells him:
'*Postponed*. The concert is postponed.'
Context also refers to the text or speech surrounding a word or phrase. The student can be asked to work out the meaning of the word by reading it in context:
*She **licked** the stamp and stuck it on the envelope.*
Assuming the student knows the other words in the sentence, he should be able to work out the meaning of *licked*.

diagnostic The teacher can use diagnostic exercises to ascertain what areas of language the student needs to practise. The student who says:

Last year I have been to Thailand. I have visited Bangkok.

is confusing the present perfect with the past simple, so the teacher might choose to incorporate work on these areas into the syllabus.

diphthongs These are phonemes. They are vowel sounds made up of two pure vowel sounds together – /eə/ in *hair* can be broken down to /e/ and /ə/.

discrimination task The student is given a choice of language items and chooses the most appropriate for the context.

He smiled kind/kindly.
Answer: *kindly.*

elicit This means *get from.* The teacher provides the idea(s), the student provides the language. If the teacher wants to find out whether or not the student knows a word, she can define it or give examples of its use to see if the student can supply the word. If he does, the teacher has succeeded in eliciting it from him.

false friends These are words which look similar to those in another language, but whose meaning is different. The student may misinterpret the word because it looks familiar: *sympathetic* could be understood to mean the same as the French *sympathique*, the Spanish *simpático* or the German *sympathisch*, all of which actually translate as *nice*.

first and third person *I* and *we* are the first person singular and plural; *he, she, it* and *they* are the third person singular and plural. It is common for learners of English to forget the third person *-s* – the verb ending in the present simple tense: *he goes, she sees, it means.*

function This is the reason for saying something. *Look out!* is a warning; the form of the verb used in *I'm seeing the dentist on Tuesday* demonstrates that it is a future arrangement; *Shall I open the window?* is an offer.

general time A verb form can refer to present, past, future or general time. General time indicates that an action is repeated or that a state which began in the past will continue into the future: *He gets up at 5.00 every day. She works in a bank.*

generative If the context used to clarify a language item is generative, several ideas can be expressed using that context – *used to* can be presented by showing a picture of a character surrounded by images of himself engaged in various activities. Each image is crossed through, indicating that he doesn't do these things any more. From these can be elicited sentences such as:

He used to smoke.
He used to drink.
He used to stay in bed until 11.00.

imperative   These verb forms are the infinitive without *to*. They may be commands, orders or instructions:
listen; sit down; be quiet; do come in.

intonation   This is the 'music' of the language, the way the voice rises and falls as a person is speaking.

kinaesthetic   Learners who access, recall and represent information to themselves in feeling and movement are kinaesthetic learners. They learn through doing and feeling.

lexis   This means vocabulary.

L1 interference   This is the term used when the errors made by the student are as a result of the influence of his own language:
I have cold to mean *I am cold.*
– a direct translation from French or Spanish.

minimal pairs   Pairs of phonemes which the student has difficulty distinguishing between are minimal pairs: Japanese speakers are often unable to hear the difference between /l/ and /r/; speakers of Latin-based languages have problems with /i:/ and /ɪ/; Arabic speakers find it difficult to hear the difference between /p/ and/b/. This is due to the fact that such sounds do not exist in their own languages, though there may be similar sounds.

modal verbs   These are a special kind of auxiliary verb such as:
will, would, can, could, may, might, must, shall, should, ought to.
They can only be used in conjunction with a main verb and can express a huge variety of functions. (Compare *I will go out later* with *I might go out later*, *I should go out later* or *I could go out later*).

morphemes   A piece of a word which affects meaning. In the word 'bees', there are two morphemes, 'bee' and 's' where plural is represented as 's'. Similarly, the word 'writing' has two morphemes, 'writ(e)' and '-ing'.

part of speech   *Noun, verb, adjective, adverb, pronoun* and so on are all parts of speech.

phoneme   This is the term given to the smallest unit of sound which can affect meaning. The three following words all share the same consonant sounds, so it is the different vowel sounds which change the meanings: *walk, work, woke*; here, it is the first consonant sound which changes the meaning: *bit, sit, kit, hit.*

phonology   The study of sounds, intonation, word and sentence stress, rhythm and aspects of connected speech is phonology. (See **intonation**, **word stress** and **sentence stress**).

pitch   This is made use of to create the music of the language in intonation. (See **intonation**.)

pure vowels   Single vowel sounds, e.g. /e/; /iː/; /ɒ/, are pure vowels.

question tags   (See **tag questions**.)

scan reading   This is the way one would read a railway timetable. Irrelevant information is ignored as the eye searches for something specific like a name or number.

sentence stress   This refers to the words of a sentence which receive the most stress or emphasis, the others being unstressed. *He told me to leave* might normally be stressed on *told* and *leave*, though there may be a reason for stressing *He* or *me*, according to the speaker's intentions. We stress the words in a sentence which are the keys to understanding.

skills   Reading, writing, speaking and listening are skills.

skim reading   This is the way one would read in order to get the gist of a text. The eye passes quickly over the whole text, so that the reader can gather the main ideas being presented or the mood of the piece. The reader can also skim to assess tone or text type.

sub-skills   Prediction, skimming/listening for gist, scanning/listening for specific information, intensive reading/listening are all sub-skills of reading and listening.

tag questions   These appear at the end of statements; they either invite the listener to comment – *It's a lovely day, isn't it?* with falling intonation – or demand confirmation – *You're from Israel, aren't you?* with rising intonation. They are also used

with suggestions or requests:
*Let's leave, **shall we?**, Have some more tea, **won't you?***

target language   This is the language the teacher is presenting to the student and wanting the student to use.

Teacher Talking Time   This refers to the time the teacher spends talking; it is not bad in itself as long as it is purposeful. Depending on the aims of an activity, it should not be at the expense of the student's talking time.

visual learners   Learners who access, recall, and represent information to themselves through images are visual learners. They learn through seeing, reading and visuals.

voiced/unvoiced sounds   These differ in that the former (e.g. /g/, /d/) make use of the voice box – vibrations can be felt by placing the hand on the throat when speaking – while the latter (e.g. /k/, /t/) do not.

word stress   This refers to which syllable of a word of more than one syllable is stressed: *canvas* is stressed on the first syllable; *exhibit* is stressed on the middle syllable and *installation* on the third. The syllable is louder and longer. The stress in a word does not change.

useful books and other materials

Oxford Advanced Learner's Dictionary (Oxford, 2000)

Collins Cobuild Learner's Dictionary (Harper Collins, 1999)

Oxford Wordpower Dictionary for Learners of English (Oxford, 2000)

Unit 1 The First Lesson

Learner English: A Teacher's Guide to Interference and Other Problems ed. Michael Swan and Bernard Smith (Cambridge University Press, 1987)

Ship or Sheep: An Intermediate Pronunciation Course Ann Baker (Cambridge University Press, 1977)

Headway Pronunciation Series Bill Bowler and Sarah Cunningham: Headway Pronunciation Pre-Intermediate (Oxford University Press, 1992); Headway Pronunciation Intermediate (Oxford University Press, 1999); Headway Pronunciation Upper Intermediate (Oxford University Press, 1991)

Business English: An Individualised Learning Programme Peter Wilberg and Michael Lewis (Language Teaching Publications, 1990). Extremely useful for business English students. It contains needs analysis sheets with a business bias, presents key business English areas of vocabulary and grammar (e.g. meetings, presentations, the telephone), and shows ways for the student to store and organize essential language.

English Grammar in Use: a self-study reference and practice book for intermediate students New Edition Raymond Murphy (Cambridge University Press, 2000). Useful for its diagnostic test – each question is cross-referenced to a unit in the book which deals with the relevant grammar area.

Essential Grammar in use: a self-study reference and practice book for elementary students of English Raymond Murphy (Cambridge University Press, 1990). A companion volume to the previous title for lower levels.

Teach Yourself English Grammar as a Second/Foreign Language John Shepheard (Hodder and Stoughton, 2001). Offers a guided discovery approach to grammar for low-level students.

Use Your Head Tony Buzan (BBC Books, 1974). This has a section on memory and recall.

Coursebooks

Advanced Masterclass CAE New Edition Tricia Aspinall and Annette Capel (Oxford University Press, 1996)

Advanced Matters Jan Bell and Roger Gower (Longman, 1999)

New First Certificate Masterclass Simon Haines and Barbara Stewart (Oxford University Press, 1994)

New Headway English Course Upper Intermediate Liz and John Soars (Oxford University Press, 1998)

Cutting Edge Upper Intermediate Sarah Cunningham and Peter Moor (Longman, 1999)

Inside Out Intermediate Sue Kay and Vaughan Jones (Macmillan Heinemann, 2000)

Cutting Edge Intermediate Sarah Cunningham and Peter Moor (Longman, 1999)

New Headway English Course Pre-Intermediate John and Liz Soars (Oxford University Press, 2000)

Pre-Intermediate Matters Jan Bell and Roger Gower (Longman, 1995)

New Headway English Course Elementary Liz and John Soars (Oxford University Press, 2000)

Elementary Matters Jan Bell and Roger Gower (Longman, 2000)

Unit 4 Learner Styles

Perfect Health: The Complete Mind/Body Guide Deepak Chopra (Harmony Books/New York, 1990). An in-depth look at the three mind-body types: *vata, pitta, kapha.*

In Your Hands: NLP in ELT Jane Revell and Sue Norman (Saffire Press, 1997). Outlines the fundamentals of Neuro-Linguistic Programming and provides a range of classroom activities inspired by NLP.

Handing Over: NLP-based activities for language learning Jane Revell and Sue Norman (Saffire Press, 1999)

Unit 6 Coursebooks, Retrospective Coursebooks and Blank Tapes

Wordflo – Your Personal English Organizer Steve Smith and Jacqueline Smith (Longman 1998). This book provides a range of ideas for organizing and recording vocabulary, grammar and pronunciation.

Unit 7 Cuisenaire Rods

Cuisenaire rods supplier:
Cuisenaire Company, 11 Crown Street, Reading RG1 2TQ.

Unit 8 Cards and Reusable Laminated Cards

The spelling game 'Anagram – the ingenious game of juggling words' is manufactured by Oxford Games Ltd., Long Crendon, Bucks, HP18 9RN.

Unit 9 Corresponding and Writing

Letters Nicky Burbidge, Peta Gray, Sheila Levy, and Mario Rinvolucri (Oxford University Press, 1997). A resource book full of ideas for exploiting letter writing.

Unit 12 Storyboard – Text Restoration

Storyboard Wida Software. The text reconstruction program.

teach yourself

teaching english
as a foreign/second language
david riddell

- are you new to teaching English?
- do you want help with planning lessons?
- are you looking for ideas and tips?

Teaching English as a Foreign Language is a practical guide
to teaching English, whether you are training to teach or new to
teaching. It gives invaluable advice and tips on effective
teaching techniques, classroom management, lesson planning,
using coursebooks, teaching different kinds of lessons, job
hunting and career development.